MW01130745

Writing Skills
for the Adolescent

Diana Hanbury King

Educators Publishing Service, Inc.
Cambridge and Toronto

Educators Publishing Service, Inc.

31 Smith Place, Cambridge, Massachusetts 02138

For Helène Durbrow
teacher extraordinary, mentor, and friend

Acknowledgments

I am indebted to all the students I have ever taught; it is from them that I have learned how to teach. I should also like to thank Shirley Kokesh, who designed some of the exercises in this book, Danny Browers of Santa Fe, without whose word-processing skills the manuscript would never have been publishable, and my mother, Una Hanbury, who provided the peace and quiet conducive to writing.

Pronoun reference in this text is primarily masculine. While this usage does reflect the distribution of the dyslexic population (dyslexia affects about seven times as many men as women), in most instances *he*, *his*, or *him* applies to both males and females and should be read as *he or she*, *his or her*, and *him or her*.

Contents

Foreword

It has been a pleasure to review this book and to formulate some of the reasons for that pleasure.

The request or suggestion to "just write it down" sounds so simple until we analyze carefully what it means. The obvious purpose of putting thoughts into writing is to convey a message, be it practical or poetic, from one mind to another. To be able to do this is a basic need in a literate, technological society such as ours. To be able to do it readily and well liberates a person to function in whatever area and role his other aptitudes and purposes suggest.

But to do it at all is the job that seems inordinately difficult, if not impossible, to many a dyslexic person. Whatever his age when we first meet him, it may be hard for him just to set pencil to paper, to form letters with reasonable fluency into legible handwriting, and to obey the simplest conventions of word and sentence structure. Beyond this are all the other skills that must be mastered, yet seem insuperable to the dyslexic faced with the demands of his academic life.

In writing, as elsewhere in the education, or re-education, of dyslexic people, we find that what seems to come easily or with only reasonable, tolerable effort for most people requires for the dyslexic special, step-by-step teaching of a particularly expert kind. Diana Hanbury King, a past master in the whole of language education of dyslexic people, is especially talented and skilled in the re-education of the *adolescent* dyslexic, who is discouragingly slowed or stopped in his academic tracks by want of the basic language skills. An important component of her success with these young people is her emphasis on their attainment and practice of writing skills, without which they cannot meet classroom and course requirements. Just how does she attain her often spectacular results?

In *Writing Skills for the Adolescent*, Mrs. King demonstrates that she, herself, can achieve what she sets as the goal for her students: to write clear, lively, informative prose that exactly serves its purpose. She explains how writing skills can best be taught, from how to hold a pencil to the use of the gerund (if you need this level of refinement). Her teaching tactics and ordering of sequences and priorities reflects a clear sense of her students' needs and interests from, as I have said elsewhere, "zero to full literacy" as they grow toward practical adulthood and, very often, college and advanced professional study. The result is a description of writing problems and her well-tested, effective response to its challenges. This makes interesting, straight-through reading that gives a quick, comprehensive, informative survey of our own language.

Its prime purpose, however, is to be a useful, practical manual in this area of teaching. It should serve both seasoned colleagues and newcomers to the field, like the many who have found teaching under Mrs. King's exacting supervision a most valuable part of their professional education and training.

Beneath the major design and all the component parts, even to the fine details of materials and procedures, moreover, one sees sound foundation. Within the specialized field of dyslexia and its treatment, Mrs. King is widely recognized as one of its very best educators. She is well-grounded in the sciences of language and language disorders. She knows psychology and pedagogy and human development. She knows the specific relations of rationale to both the subject matter to be taught and the real live, lively teenage boys, and sometimes girls, who people her school and camp. You know that behind prescription or suggestion there is not whim but valid and tested reason.

Users of this book should find themselves enjoying the zest that accompanies the variety, timeliness, and frequent humor that it both supplies and suggests as part of the hard work and adherence to the high but realistic standards it requires. (Students should do their very best, she believes, but some mistakes are inevitable. We are educating dyslexics, "not training secretaries.")

Hundreds of students have helped develop the methodology for her approach. Their remediation involves some grueling labor and sometimes discouragement, but they feel rewarded in the end by having achieved a sense of genuine improvement, often of fluent, effective competence in the use of the written word to serve in the pursuit of their several life purposes.

Teachers of writing should find *Writing Skills for the Adolescent* of value with any student of English writing but especially with the young people whose needs it directly addresses.

MARGARET BYRD RAWSON

1. Introduction

Writing is thinking in slow motion. We see what at normal speeds escapes us, can rerun the reel at will to look for errors, erase, interpolate, and rethink. Most thoughts are a light rain, fall upon the ground, and dry up. Occasionally they become a stream that runs a short distance before it disappears. Writing stands an incomparably better chance of getting somewhere.

Paintings and sculptures are also new worlds, but confined by space; and if the artist wants many people to share them, he must part with his works. What is written can be given endlessly and yet retained, read by thousands even while it is being rewritten, kept as it was and revised at the same time. Writing is magic. —Walter Kaufman, *Tragedy and Philosophy*

By adolescence, most dyslexics have learned to read. In some instances, several months or years of tutoring have enabled them at least to break the code. Others seem to learn to read almost spontaneously without much in the way of specialized teaching, not, to be sure, at age five or six, but at eleven or twelve. A third group, less profoundly dyslexic, may have difficulty from the beginning with only the written word and may read fluently even before first grade. Decoding may be weak and oral reading inaccurate, but all these students can certainly read with good, or even excellent, comprehension.

This ability to read places these students under extraordinary pressures. Teachers know they are bright. They are responsive and intelligent during class discussion and, besides, their intelligence has been tested. Since they can read, obviously they cannot be dyslexic, for relatively few teachers understand that dyslexia means difficulty with language in *all* its aspects—speech, reading, writing, spelling, and foreign language. Why then, wonder teachers, does an intelligent youngster refuse to write, deliberately misspell words (surely any fifteen year old cannot be ignorant of the correct spelling of *they* and *which*), and scribble so that no one can read his writing? Why doesn't he remember to capitalize even when he remembers to use periods? He sits in class, too lazy to take notes even if they are put on the board to copy, and always has some excuse for failing to produce assigned papers. What he does turn in is an insult to his teachers. When required to recopy work, he seems to add new errors. Labelled lazy, careless, and slovenly, he disappoints his teachers, his parents, and himself.

Many years ago, I tested two boys, aged twelve and fourteen. Their mother brought them to my house on a clear, sunny day. By the time we had shaken hands, I realized that both of them were terrified. They were so frightened that I did not know which to test first. On principle, I started with the older one. Both boys scored above a twelfth-grade level on all the reading tests. When we came to the spelling, neither could do better than a third- or fourth-grade level. It was not until about a year later when we were off riding horses on the trail that I said, "Remember the time you came to my house and I tested you? You seemed to be so uptight, and I've always wondered why." Then I found out that they had already been tested at a university reading clinic. The psychologist who had administered the battery of tests had called them into his office and said, "You boys certainly must hate your parents to be doing this to them." They were waiting for the moment when I would make a similar comment. So it is, that in many instances the brighter and more competent the student, the greater the pressure for written work.

Of course writing skills are crucial for success in high school and college, but there are other reasons for teaching writing. Writing is a way of strengthening memory. All of us have had the experience of arriving at the grocery store and realizing that the carefully planned shopping list is sitting at home on the kitchen table. But it does not really matter because the process of writing it down fixed it in the memory. Once I worked with a student on whom the experts from the local school system had given up. He could never remember anything. Whatever he learned, he forgot. And no wonder, for he had no way of writing things down in order to fix them in his memory. Once he learned to write, his prospects changed.

Writing is a way of capturing our own thoughts, of finding out what we think, and perhaps even why we think it. Ideas flash through our minds. They flow down the stream of consciousness and are lost. The writing process slows the stream down and diverts it into a pool in which we can glimpse ourselves. The practice of writing improves thinking skills. Learning to organize our own writing helps us to understand the writings of others; reading comprehension improves.

Writing can also be viewed as a creative outlet for the imagination. Perhaps just because the dyslexic has to struggle with words, he may develop unusual facility with poetic imagery more readily than those of us who have grown up taking our language for granted. The list of famous dyslexics includes Hans Christian Andersen, F. Scott Fitzgerald, Amy Lowell, and Robert Frost.

Of course, not all students can aspire to become writers or even to attend college. On the other end of the scale is the despair and embarrassment suffered by the dyslexic who cannot write at all. I remember one young man who was enjoying his work at a service station—he had pretty good mechanical aptitude—until the owner asked him to go into the back room and inventory the tires. Rather than reveal his inability to write, he slipped away and never returned. On another occasion, a young adult with whom a colleague and I had worked successfully for a year or so called us in a panic. In the trucking business, he had been offered a promotion, but the job would require that he keep a log. We advised him to talk the problem over with his boss. The latter, for whom a special place in heaven should be reserved, remarked, "Well, in my experience, guys that can spell can't drive trucks," and offered him the job anyway.

There are at least two reasons why teachers fail to tackle writing skills. First, they are not sure where to begin when faced with a jumble of illegibly-written, poorly-constructed, misspelled sentences—or, perhaps worse, with the student who stares at the paper for ten minutes and can think of nothing to write. This book attempts to offer a solution in the form of a structured approach that begins with the small, simple unit and goes on to tackle the longer and more complex, in the fashion we naturally proceed in the teaching of mathematics, chemistry, physics, or even biology. At no stage is the student faced with a task he cannot perform; learning proceeds from the simple to the complex.

Another reason why teachers hesitate is that they do not realize how much can be accomplished in a short time. Writing samples included in the appendix illustrate the extent of the progress that is possible. Because improvement is rapid, students are encouraged by the results of their efforts and motivated to persist.

While the material in this book is designed for use in the classroom or with small groups, it can be readily used by tutors. Moreover, while it is intended for adolescents, most of the exercises, especially those on paragraph structure, have been used successfully with fourth and fifth graders. It is not a workbook; the exercises are merely springboards that the teacher or tutor can use as models to develop other drills appropriate to the age and interests of the individual or group. Some groups may enjoy making up exercises with which to challenge their fellow students.

The chapters should be presented in overlapping fashion. For instance, while sentence writing needs to be carried on over a long period of time, exercises that involve devising supporting sentences for a given topic can be started almost from the beginning. Similarly, perfection in writing single paragraphs of all sorts need not be attained before beginning essay writing. Spelling must be practiced daily, but poor spelling must not be allowed to become a barrier that inhibits progress in other areas or compels the student to languish in boredom, denied the opportunity of exercising his wit and imagination.

2. Handwriting

Teaching, especially of dyslexics, must be multisensory. These days, the word *modality* is in vogue. But, paradoxically, nobody seems to pay much attention to the teaching of handwriting. Rapid, legible, and comfortable handwriting is important for success in high school and college. But more than that, it is almost a prerequisite for teaching reading to the dyslexic. It is the kinesthetic sense, the feeling of the movement, that fixes the letters in one's memory. Writing is needed to reinforce the reading. Maria Montessori noticed that young children make attempts at writing before they read—and anybody who has young children can observe the same thing. Too little attention is paid to the teaching of writing in the early grades, and none at all later on. Few teachers seem to know what to do about it, other than asking students to recopy their work, sometimes repeatedly. Yet—and this is a useful statement to make to students—handwriting affects every grade a student receives, for papers are corrected, not by machines, but by tired teachers, often at the end of the day or late at night, and the illegible or messy paper inevitably receives less credit.

Writing difficulties often begin before first grade. Young children get a fist grip on the pencil—and who on earth ever decided that those tiny fingers should be given thick kindergarten pencils the size of fence posts! Then too, the horizontal shape of the paper commonly used in elementary grades makes it impossible for the elbow to pivot, and digital muscles become overused from the beginning.

In the first grade, many dyslexic students learn to form the letters incorrectly. It is interesting to observe that dyslexics often draw a person by beginning with the feet and working upwards; they'll do the same with letters, particularly manuscript *f*, *l*, *h*, *p*, *r*, and *t*—letters that do not begin on the line. The recent technique of forming the letters *a*, *b*, *d*, *g*, *p*, and *q* with two strokes, sticks and balls, exacerbates matters. As one youngster remarked to me, "*a*, *b*, *c*, *d*—they're all the same," and for him they really were.

I do not know and have never been able to discover just who decided that students should print for the first two and a half years of their school life. The rationale is, of course, that the early introduction of cursive writing would confuse children since they would be dealing with two sets of symbols. I might have believed this but for the fact that my first teaching job was at the Ruzawi School in Southern Rhodesia. There, I taught the first form of sixteen seven-year-old boys. They already knew how to write, having been taught mostly at home on the farms from which they came. Their cursive writing was of a form and size that we would expect of our fourth graders—no double-lined paper either. European students develop elegant cursive writing in the early grades. They show no signs of confusing manuscript and cursive letter forms. Nor should they, for writing is a kinesthetic process, dealing with the feeling of movement, whereas reading is visual—looking at the words.

There is no reason why cursive writing should not be taught from the beginning to all students. However, in the case of dyslexics, there are several reasons for insisting on cursive. To begin with, in cursive writing there is no question as to where each letter begins—it begins *on* the line. The confusion with forms is not merely a left and right reversal as with *b/d* and *p/q*; it is also an up and down reversal as with *m/w* and *u/n*; hence the uncertainty as to whether a letter begins at the top or the bottom. Second, spelling is fixed more firmly in the mind if the word is formed in a continuous movement rather than in a series of separate strokes with the pencil lifted off the paper between each one.

Many adolescents still print. Some of them

come from private schools where calligraphy has been in fashion—a disaster for young dyslexics. At one private school, I watched fourth-grade boys struggle to learn the thick and thin strokes with two pencils tied together. Even for the better writers, elegance is achieved at the expense of speed. Although most dyslexics learn to print in first grade, when the transition to cursive is made in third grade, they never quite learn it correctly. Watch carefully and you can notice some odd cursive formations, especially letters such as *a*, *d*, *g*, *p*, and *q* made with the circles going in the wrong direction. Dyslexics often fail to master the capitals altogether. Teachers cannot understand why they do not capitalize, but the fact of the matter is that they are never quite sure of the letter formations. A particular dyslexic trait is the reversal at the beginning of cursive capital letters such as *l*, *m*, *n*, and *w* where the beginning loop is reversed, resulting in a shape like a lowercase *o*. Incidentally, if you are asked to diagnose dyslexia on the basis of a handwriting sample, this is one of the signs to watch for. Thus, the dyslexic often fails to master cursive and writes illegibly. Sooner or later a teacher remarks, "Why don't you print? At least I'd be able to read it," and, with a sigh of relief, the student reverts to printing. Often this printing is an indiscriminate mixture of lower- and uppercase letters.

It is always worth the trouble to go back and develop good writing skills. True dysgraphia is very rare indeed although the diagnosis is often made. With older students, dramatic results can be achieved with a short period of intensive

Figure 1.

Not sufficiently slanted

Slanted too far

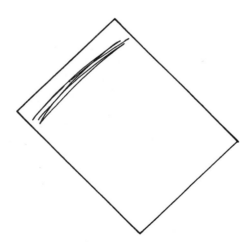

Correct for right-handed student

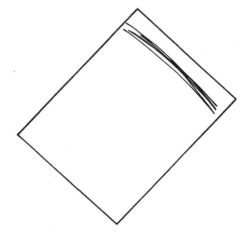

Correct for left-handed student

Figure 2.

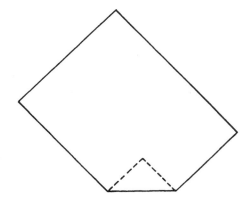

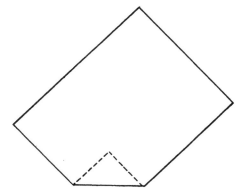

Paper positioned for
right-handed student

Paper positioned for
left-handed student

training, and the results invariably repay the effort. Even a week of daily work can make enough difference to encourage a student to continue with what may have initially seemed a pointless exercise, or an awkward change of position, and two weeks will almost always produce clear, legible script. The requisite speed will then come with further practice. However, it *must* be a period in which he is writing only under the supervision of a teacher. If he spends an hour a day with a tutor, then proceeds to revert to his old habits during the rest of the day, the expected results may not be achieved. It is sometimes necessary to find the time during a school vacation period, or to make a special arrangement with the school.

GRIP, POSITION, AND POSTURE

So, where do we begin with adolescents whose handwriting or printing is illegible? The place to begin is with posture and pencil grip. Do not begin with letter formation. During the period when new habits are being established, use scribbling exercises.

Paper position is crucial. The paper must be slanted at a forty-five-degree angle—no more and no less. The hand must swing across the paper using the elbow as a pivot. If the paper is slanted too much, the words will fall below the line; if not

enough, they will fly off it. (See Figure 1.) Strips of tape attached to the desk like train tracks can help maintain the correct position. Another trick, invented by a student of mine, is to turn under the corner of the paper. The resulting edge is then kept parallel to the edge of the table. (See Figure 2.)

Posture is important. Students need to learn to sit up straight. They spend hours in school sitting at desks, often hunched over in a position that makes proper breathing impossible. Any student, especially one interested in athletics, can be shown how to breathe deeply from the diaphragm. He should be instructed to place both hands over the front of the chest just below the rib cage and then to take a deep breath, feeling the lungs expand. Another way of illustrating this point is to have the student sit in a hunched over position and then instruct him to take a deep breath—impossible, of course.

Both elbows should be on the table at all times during a tutoring session. Thus, the elbows and the head form a triangle, and the student is ready to work. (See Figure 3.) In addition, this position stabilizes the head and there is less head movement during reading. Head swinging during reading can be further controlled by having the student place both hands on the side of the head, producing even greater stability. At first, reminders as to correct posture may need to be frequent: touching the elbow lightly is sufficient. Incidentally, for tutoring purposes, the teacher should sit at a forty-five-degree angle to the

Figure 3.

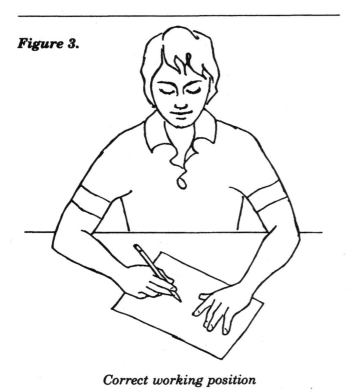

Correct working position

student. (See Figure 4.) In this position he or she can easily watch the writing of the student. Too often neglected are the size and height of the tutoring table—less than five feet by three feet is too small. The student's feet should be on the floor; use a box or stool if necessary. Young children cannot be expected to learn to write properly on a table that comes up to their chins or seated on a chair that leaves their feet dangling.

Pencil grip must be properly established. The thumb and index finger grip the pencil, and the third finger supports it from below. The pencil rests in the hollow between thumb and forefinger, and the eraser points toward the shoulder. Probably the most common error is that of holding the pencil between the thumb and third finger with the index finger resting idly on top, allowing the pencil to slip. Occasionally a student will have developed a habit of writing with the pencil between the index and third fingers. Another faulty position, which has been termed the simian grip, uses all five fingers together. Triangular pencil grippers or the Zaner-Blozer writing frame are helpful in establishing this initial position. The wrist should be kept fairly flat so that the arm can pivot on the forearm muscle. Have your student roll up his sleeve and show him which muscle you are talking about.

PRE-WRITING EXERCISES

With the foregoing established, you are ready to begin a series of exercises. The first of these is a windshield wiper back and forth across the page. (See Figure 5.) As the student writes, the non-writing hand rests at the top of the paper and moves it upward between two imaginary tracks. This hand serves the same function as the roller on a typewriter, moving the paper upward so that the writing hand can remain in the same position. Too often we see a student trying to write with one hand in his lap and the paper sliding around, or writing to the bottom of the page with his arms dangling off the edge of the desk. Both elbows should be on the table all the time. (See Figure 6.)

Figure 4.

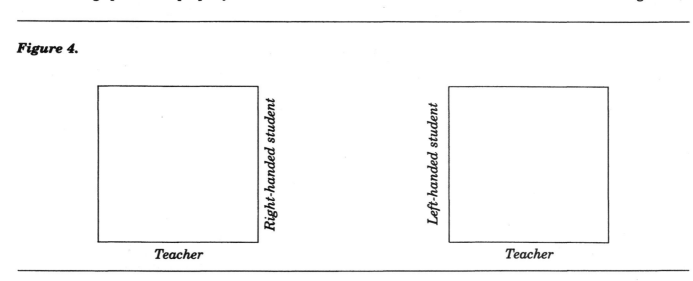

Right-handed student

Teacher

Left-handed student

Teacher

Figure 5.

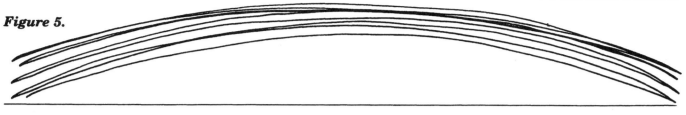

Figure 6.

Correct for right-handed student

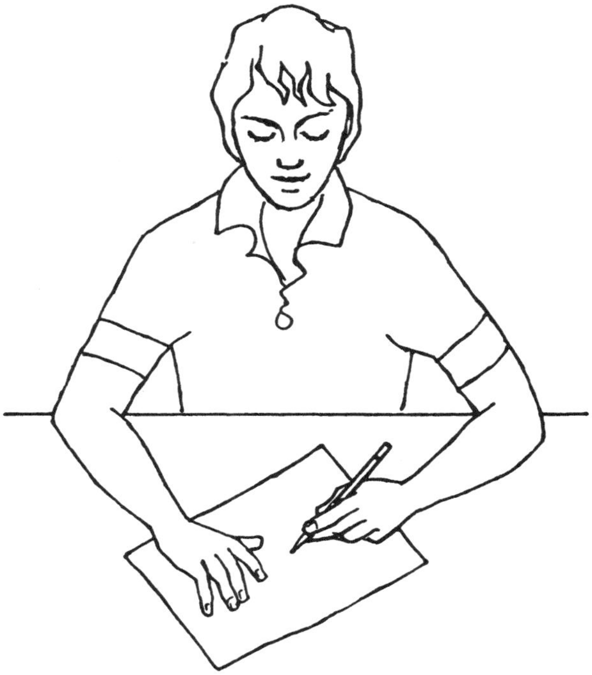

Correct for left-handed student

Incorrect

Standing behind your student, you can place your hand over his hand, positioning his wrist and fingers correctly. Get him to close his eyes and feel the proper position of arm, wrist, and fingers. As soon as he can do this, continue the series of scribbling exercises with the wind tunnel, in whichever direction seems easier. (See Figure 7.) The next step is to tighten it up, keeping the circles round. (See Figure 8.) During this exercise, the digital muscles should be merely holding the pencil—the work is done by the large arm muscle. This exercise can be difficult. The arm and posture need to be relaxed—sometimes closing or averting the eyes helps. Next comes the push-pull exercise. (See Figure 9.) It should be followed by Figure 10, and then the more difficult Figure 11.

The latter were devised in England by Marion Richardson in her series of books, *Writing and Writing Patterns** and can be combined in various ways. (See Figure 12.) Other possibilities based on different patterns include those in Figure 13. These seemingly simple exercises are surprisingly difficult; in fact, a fifteen- or sixteen-year-old may be quite unable to do them. But until he can manage them in relaxed fashion, comfortably and easily, letter formation will have to wait.

Figure 7.

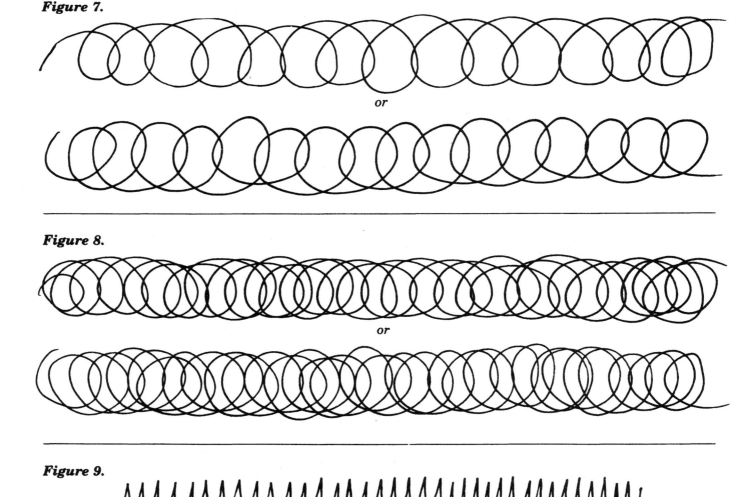

or

Figure 8.

or

Figure 9.

*Marion Richardson, *Writing and Writing Patterns* (Sevenoaks, Kent, England: Hodder and Stoughton Educational, n.d.)

Figure 10.

Figure 11.

Figure 12.

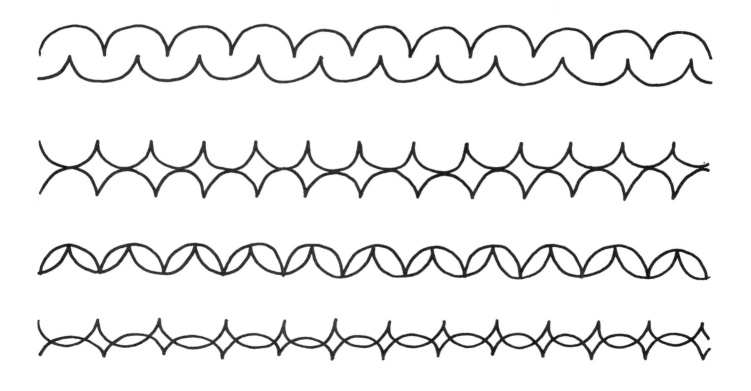

Figure 12 (continued)

Figure 13.

THE LEFT-HANDED STUDENT

The left-handed student often starts with an added handicap—that of writing with a hooked wrist. This position, which I once heard the great Anna Gillingham term "a monument to the ig- norance or laziness of teachers" is always worth correcting, even in a young adult. Sometimes it is reasoned that "his writing looks fine, so why bother?" However, this position, which forces the tendon to stretch over two joints, ultimately creates strain and tension. It is true that many adults write in this fashion. Often at restaurants and in stores, I watch waiters or clerks struggle to write up my check or sales slip with wrist hooked and I'm tempted to say, "I could show you. . . ." The rapid writing required of students in college or high school requires a speed and facility that cannot be achieved in this position. Once, at summer camp, a young counselor watched us work and changed his writing of his own accord. When he returned the following summer, he said, "For the first time, I've been able to take all the notes I needed." This faulty wrist position can become deeply entrenched, and it is essential to be firm about getting it straight. It should be corrected immediately from the first—not gradually. Once the correct position has been established, the student cannot be allowed to revert even briefly.

The position of the paper for the left-handed is the mirror image of that for the right-handed. (See Figure 14.) *Always* the writing should slant backhand, away from the body. The initial scribbling exercises should be done backhand, too. (See Figure 15.)

Some right-handed students should write with a backhand slant. Often this can be decided on the basis of the initial scribbling exercises, but there are a couple of other considerations, too. First of all, some students who are right-handed but left-eyed will do better writing backhand. Then it is often good, even as a temporary corrective measure, for those right-handed students who have developed the habit of writing by flipping their wrists back and forth so that their writing develops an excessive forward slant. (See Figure 16.) Writing backhand will force them to bring another set of muscles into play.

Persuading an adolescent to change away from the conventional is not usually difficult. Careful observation of school papers, especially those written hastily, will often provide the necessary clues as to the most natural and comfortable slant. A student whose writing slopes in various directions, or one who has not succeeded in establishing a righthand slant, despite years of practice, may well be more comfortable writing backhand. Sometimes, straight-up-and-down writing may be the most comfortable and legible. The three criteria for good handwriting—legibility, speed, and comfort—must always be kept in mind.

Figure 14.

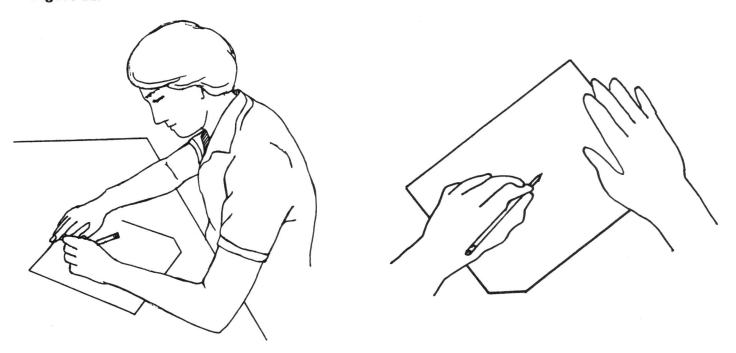

Correct paper position for left-handed student

Figure 15.

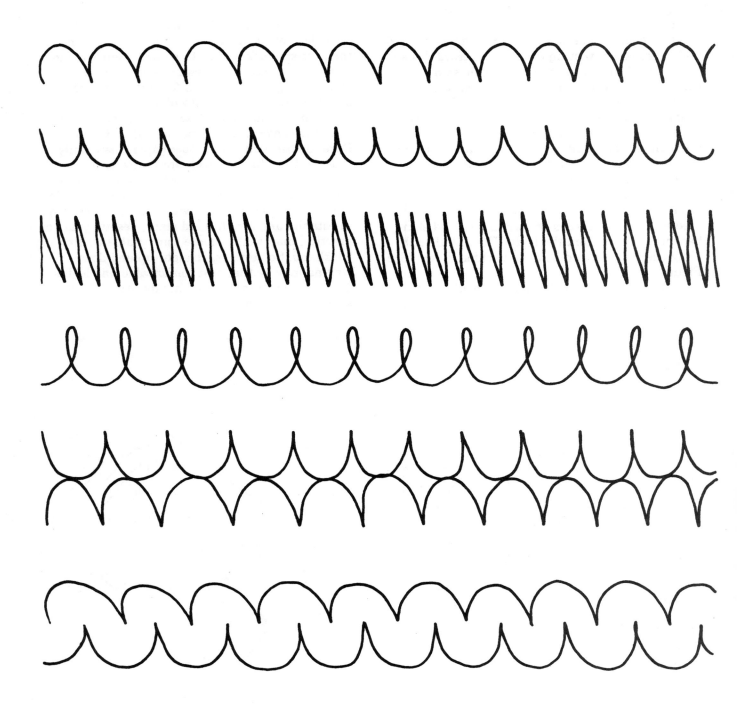

Figure 16.

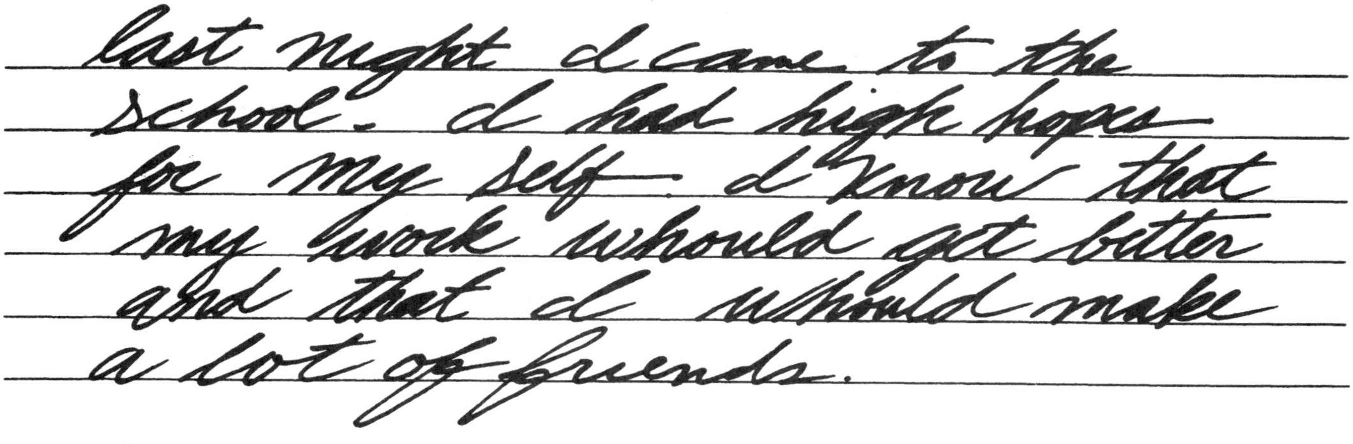

last night I came to the school. I had high hopes for my self I know that my work whould get better and that I whould make a lot of friends.

FORMATION OF LOWERCASE LETTERS

Once students have established the correct grip, writing position, and posture, it is time to work on letter formation. Adolescents do not need to learn letters in groups nor do they need specially lined paper. Unless they are having difficulty with formation of a particular letter, they do not need to write large. Skipping lines, though, is always helpful and should be continued for some time into the remediation process.

Teach individual letters first, always with an upstroke and an ending stroke. There are two kinds of upstroke. (See Figure 17.) If the upstrokes are not properly taught, illegible formations will result. (See Figure 18.) Failure to teach ending strokes results in improperly joined letters. (See Figure 19.) Never ask a student to write a whole line of one letter. Three or five should be the most required. (See Sample Worksheet 1.) Students should be encouraged to trace first, then to copy, always starting on the line. In your models, be careful not to exaggerate the ending strokes, as your students will exaggerate them even more.

Figure 17.

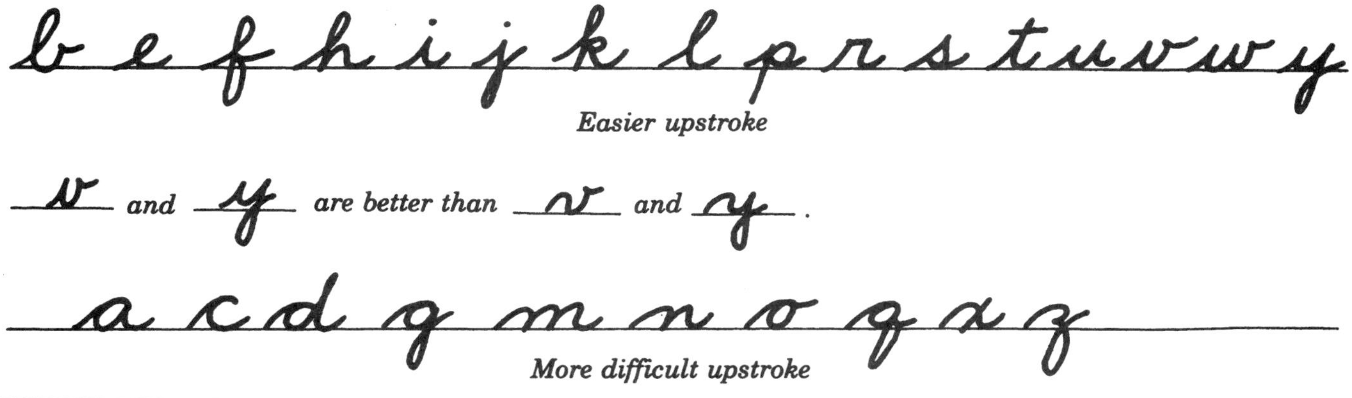

b e f h i j k l p r s t u v w y

Easier upstroke

___ and ___ are better than ___ and ___.

a c d g m n o q x z

More difficult upstroke

Figure 18.

Incorrect upstrokes

Figure 19.

Incorrect ending strokes

Figure 20.

Correct
ending stroke

Exaggerated
ending stroke

Figure 21.

Misformed letters

(See Figure 20.) Certain letters can be particularly difficult. Despite its simple appearance, *o* is often troublesome and its malformation results in endless difficulties and confusion with *a*. These two letters are not round so much as oval. The *o* stops at midnight; the *a*, at two o'clock. Another tricky letter is *k*. Too often, students misform the group of letters *l*, *h*, *k*, and *f* by letting the letter cross on the line. (See Figure 21.) Left-handed students often cross a *t* from right to left, just as they make \ for √. Once established, there is no need to correct this natural tendency. For the dyslexic, *m* and *n* are a source of endless confusion. This is in part because of the similarity of the nasal sounds, though *m* is made with lips together and *n* with lips parted. But even worse is the confusion created by the printed formations *n* and *m* and the four bridge letters *b*, *o*, *v*, and *w*. Thus, *om* is written for *on* and, conversely, many letters home begin *Dear Mon*. Appropriate exercises have to be devised for these misformations.

Once the letter shapes have been mastered, it is time to begin alphabet practice. Never teach students to join an alphabet; it is a pointless exercise. (See Figure 22.) Letters, all with their proper upstrokes and ending strokes, should be carefully formed and spaced on two lines. Skip a line between each alphabet. (See Sample Worksheet 2.)

For a long time, probably a year, tutoring lessons should begin with the alphabet sequence—lowercase and, later, uppercase as well. Where there are problems, it is often best to work with one or two letters at a time. From time to time, the student should be timed in his writing of an alphabet, and the improvement noted.

Two other important techniques, kinesthetic writing and simultaneous oral spelling, help the development of the motor memory crucial to the learning of spelling. Kinesthetic writing is writing with eyes averted. This technique is important for copying from a chalkboard. Skilled writers copy from the board with only an occasional glance at the paper to position the hand. It was Katrina de

Figure 22.

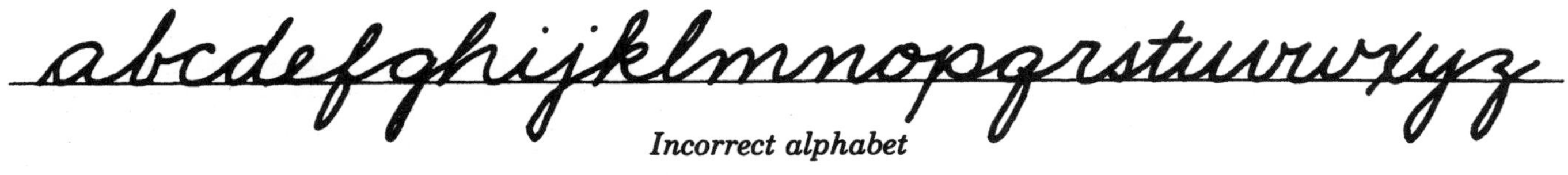

Incorrect alphabet

Hirsch who first taught me how closing down one of the senses makes the others more acute. She used to tell the story of a little girl who had difficulty in learning how to put on a coat. When she was blindfolded, she quickly mastered the movement, and was, of course, always able to do it after that. If we want to listen carefully, to judge the quality of a sound, to tell whether or not someone is lying, it is helpful to avert the eyes. Teaching a child to write with eyes averted or closed not only strengthens the motor pattern, but it also relaxes the muscles. Another useful technique is to hold a sheet of stiff paper between the student and the work.

Simultaneous Oral Spelling (the Gillingham S.O.S. device) provides another form of kinesthetic reinforcement in which movement of the speech organs helps the memory. As the student forms the letter, he says its name aloud—always the name rather than the sound. Teachers often cannot be bothered to do this, and older students are often self-conscious, reluctant, or downright rebellious. But, with some explanation and with firm insistence, most of them will adopt the technique during tutorial sessions.

In *Letters from an Actor*, William Redfield says, "Most observers say to actors, 'How do you remember all those lines?' " and then he goes on to

Sample Worksheet 2.

a b c d e f g h i j k l m

n o p q r s t u v w x y z

1.

2.

3.

quote Marlon Brando:

> I am good when I forget. When I can sit on stage
> and think of catching a fish. I have just sunk the
> hook, there's a tug on the line, and at that
> preoccupied moment I hear my cue. My God, what
> is my line? And then I say my line, because the
> motor memory will save you if you really believe.
> So I say my line, the line I thought I'd forgotten,
> and it's good, man. It's really good.*

This motor memory is indeed a powerful device, and one which we cannot afford to deny our student if he is to learn to spell. Writing is not drawing; it is not a visual process, but a movement that must become automatic if it is to be useful.

Once students have mastered individual letters, move on to short words or syllables. This is likely to be the stage at which teacher and student are working with single syllables and short-vowel discrimination. Units should be short and written down the page in a column. Too long a writing task can cause newly established handwriting skills to deteriorate. Difficult combinations with bridge letters or *m/n* and *a/o* confusions can be worked on at this stage. Sometimes the four "finish-later letters," *i, j, t,* and *x* need practice. The writer should not interrupt the motor pattern

* William Redfield, *Letters from an Actor* (New York: Limelight Editions, 1966), p. 60.

in mid-word to dot an *i* or cross a *t*. This may also be the time to sort out the *b/d* confusion that can persist into adolescence in the case of the severely dyslexic. Anna Gillingham used to suggest putting a picture of a boy on one side of the tutoring room and a duck on the other. But this is a visual clue, and a kinesthetic one will be stronger. In the early stages of manuscript, "*b* is tall and has a ball" and "first the drum and then the stick" work well. But for older students learning cursive, "*d* starts like *a*" suffices to sort out the pair.

FORMATION OF CAPITAL LETTERS

Only when lowercase letters have been well established should capitals be tackled. Capitals are difficult. Many students fail to capitalize because they are uncertain of the formation of capital letters. A dyslexic adult once told me that his most difficult year in school was seventh grade. Throughout the first six grades, the black and white alphabet charts hung above the chalkboard and he could always refresh his memory with a swift glance. Then, in seventh grade they were gone.

Capital letters are difficult because their forms are convoluted and they begin in different places—on the line or above it, and in different directions. For example, capital *i* begins on the line and goes backwards; capital *d* begins above the line and goes down; capital *l* begins above the line and goes forward. Dyslexics, who have directional difficulties, find these letters extraordinarily confusing. Adolescents do not need to learn capitals in groups, but they do need many practice sheets carefully prepared for the individual slope and, at first, marked with the starting place. Troublesome letter formations may have to be traced first. The teacher should make the model to be traced large and the pattern should be traced repeatedly. (See Figure 23.)

Some students may need specially prepared worksheets for capitals. At first, indicate both place and direction of the starting stroke with an arrow. (See Sample Worksheet 3.) Later, a dot will suffice as a clue. (See Sample Worksheet 4.) Next, students should write complete alphabets of capitals, as they did with lowercase letters. (See Sample Worksheet 5.) Finally, students should practice capitals in words. (See Sample Worksheet 6.)

Figure 23.

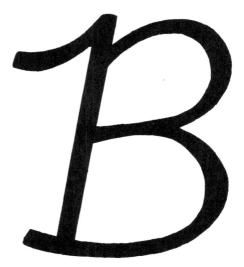

A chalkboard is of little use in teaching writing to the adolescent because it brings a different set of muscles into play. But using the table top as a writing surface provides an excellent motor exercise. Letters should be formed with the whole hand and be several inches high. Writing the capitals in this fashion can be a relaxing exercise and is a good method of making sure their forms are established forever.

Correct formation of numerals should be included at the same time. Even older students often misform the two-stroke numerals *4* and *5* and have trouble with *8* ("starts at the top like *S*").

TYPING

Typing is an important skill, but it is not a substitute for writing. It forms yet another avenue for kinesthetic reinforcement. All college students should be able to type and, increasingly, to use a word processor, as well as a computer. The conventional methods of teaching typing simply do not work well for the dyslexic, and the hunt-and-peck method is inefficient. Far too many dyslexic students fail to learn in typing schools and courses, and the computer typing courses available are improperly designed. This is unfortunate, as with proper teaching, any ten-year old can master the keyboard in about half an hour. But it must be taught as a motor process, not a visual one. Teach it by way of the alphabet. Eyes should be closed or

Sample Worksheet 3.

averted, though when students work with a computer, their eyes can be fixed on the monitor. Blank keys, or keys painted out or capped are helpful, but not essential.

Begin by explaining to the student the significance of a conditioned reflex—perhaps using the classic case of the bell and the salivating dog. Then tell him that every time his finger hits a letter, he is going to name the letter in order to make a connection. If he does so faithfully over a period of time, the mere naming of the letter will cause the correct finger to move. Eventually, just thinking of the letter will produce the same response.

Position the fingers on the home keys *(asdf–jkl;)*. It may be helpful to mark these with a tiny piece of tape. Some typewriters now have a small raised dot on the home keys. If you wish, you can, as a preliminary exercise, teach the student to type his first name. Then begin with the alphabet. Teach "*a*, reach for *b*" by moving the student's index finger from *f* to *b*. After touching *b* the index finger returns quickly to its home key. Practice until this is easy, ten or twenty times. The next sequence, *c d e*, is done with the middle finger. Once this is mastered, do the entire sequence—*a b c d e*—always naming each letter *aloud*. Continue adding a group of letters and practicing it until it

Sample Worksheet 4.

has been mastered, then going back to the beginning of the alphabet and putting the entire sequence together. Add letters in groups as follows:

a b	*a*, reach for *b*
c d e	middle finger
f g	
h i	
j k l	3 in a row
m n	you're halfway there
o	ring finger up
p q	little fingers
r s t	the most difficult sequence of all will need extra time
u v	index fingers up and down
w x	both fourth fingers—*x* is awkward, but how often do you need it?
y	reach for it
z	

After half an hour or so your student will be typing the entire alphabet and eager for more. Do allow him to spend some time playing around.

$$\mathcal{A} \; \mathcal{B} \; \mathcal{C} \; \mathcal{D} \; \mathcal{E} \; \mathcal{F} \; \mathcal{G} \; \mathcal{H} \; \mathcal{I} \; \mathcal{J} \; \mathcal{K} \; \mathcal{L} \; \mathcal{M}$$

$$\mathcal{N} \; \mathcal{O} \; \mathcal{P} \; \mathcal{Q} \; \mathcal{R} \; \mathcal{S} \; \mathcal{T} \; \mathcal{U} \; \mathcal{V} \; \mathcal{W} \; \mathcal{X} \; \mathcal{Y} \; \mathcal{Z}$$

1.

2.

3.

Continue the alphabet practice with twenty or thirty alphabets daily. As this practice begins to become boring, introduce some variations. Teach the use of the space bar by having the student type *a* space *b* space *c* space *d*, etc. He should, of course, say *space* as he hits the space bar. This can be followed by *a* comma space *b* comma space *c* comma space *d*, etc. and by *a* period space space *b* period space space *c* period space space *d* period space space, etc., thereby establishing that a comma is always followed by a single space and a period by a double space.

As the student gains confidence and skill, begin to pay more attention to correct posture and finger position. Too much fussing about this at the beginning can be discouraging. Do continue to insist on hearing him name each letter as his fingers move, at least for the first month. By then he will be typing sentences and letters to friends.

Take words from a list of common words—

Sample Worksheet 6.

And	Not
But	Over
Can	Put
Do	Quick
Ever	Run
For	Stop
Go	To
He	Up
In	Very
Just	We
Kit	Xylem
Let	Yes
Man	Zest

the, and, me, we, be, she, your, they, on, over, up, from, far, inside, outside, only, all, always, never— and have him write a line of each word. He will soon discover that his fingers will feel it when he makes a mistake. During this stage, teach him to retype an entire word when an error occurs, so that the entire motor pattern is repeated. Capital letters come next, and the student can begin to compose short sentences. At some point, you can introduce numerals, in order, and then other symbols as needed. If you have never tried this before, you will find the experience as rewarding as your student will, and you will be eager to do it again. It is fun, and it always works.

Recently a parent told me that he had given his son a computer but had insisted that he could not touch it until he had mastered touch typing. So far, the boy did not have access to the computer despite hours of practice. I asked, "And how long has he been trying to learn?" "Three months." Imagine the disappointment and frustration, and all of it quite unnecessary.

3. The Sentence

ACHIEVING SENTENCE VARIETY

For the dyslexic, sentence writing provides an important transition between single words and paragraphs and essays. The adolescent dyslexic has done very little writing in his life. What success he has experienced in school has been achieved by filling blanks, successfully matching and dealing with multiple choice questions on tests and exams, and by contributing intelligently to class discussion. Writing has been a threatening activity to be avoided at all costs. It is therefore important that the initial writing assignments be designed to build his confidence. Begin with single sentences. An assignment that requires him to use ten or twenty or even thirty words in a sentence is, at worst, tedious. It is not likely to be something he feels he cannot do. It is important to provide the dyslexic with a great deal of writing practice. His peers have acquired facility by dint of covering hundreds of pages with writing. He needs much practice in order to establish newly acquired handwriting skills and to begin to improve spelling. Because the sentence unit is a short one, he will be more likely to spell a given word correctly in a sentence than in a paragraph.

But there is another reason for practicing writing. Often the dyslexic will be found gazing off into space. When a proctor suggests that he needs to get on with his work, the reply is likely to be, "I'm thinking. I'm trying to think of a sentence for this word." Those of us who are fluent writers manage the two processes simultaneously. There seems to be a flow from brain to pen and only rarely do we pause. I have discussed this with several writers, who feel as I do that they are merely writing down what something inside them dictates. This fluent transfer of ideas into words on paper is acquired through practice. Formulating ideas on paper is not the same as formulating sentences in speech.

First, elicit sentences in conjunction with the teaching of spelling—perhaps a list of *oi/oy* and *ou/ow* words to be copied and then used in sentences in order to reinforce particular sounds as they are introduced. Writing on alternate lines is important as it facilitates correct spelling and ultimately, proofreading, and should be established as a habit from the first.

The fashion in which the teacher reacts to these sets of sentences is important. For at least a year, and probably longer, nothing a dyslexic writes should be marked with a red pen; papers should be marked lightly in pencil or black pen, if at all. No dyslexic has ever learned to spell from seeing a paper covered with "sp." or with the correct spelling written above the misspelled word. What he does learn is discouragement and sometimes despair. When I first started teaching fifth grade at Sidwell Friends School in 1950, I used to take home stacks of papers every night and painstakingly correct every single error, feeling that to miss any would be to have someone consider me a lazy, careless teacher. If you are teaching a dyslexic, his error is a signal to you that something needs to be taught or drilled further.

Never correct all the mistakes on a page—in fact, do not even tell your student about most of them. Never, never say, "And what on earth is this sentence?" If you cannot decipher it, keep that fact to yourself. Perhaps at first, all you will do is insist on a capital letter at the beginning and a period, or some other form of punctuation, at the end. You do not want your student to be inhibited by his inability to spell a word. Your goal is to loosen the dam, to unleash some expression. Comment positively on content, on humor, on sentence length. Read the best aloud and say, "I really like that sentence," or "That's a neat sentence," and the sentences will improve steadily. After a few days, begin to collect the common words misspelled—*thay, wus, frome, whith, whitch*— and place them on three-by-five cards for repeated drill. Select increasing numbers of words from the student's writing vocabulary to be written for practice, incorporated into sentences, and dictated daily.

Once he has acquired some facility, set about improving the quality of his sentences. Most students begin their sentences with *I*. A list of possible beginning words from which to choose is helpful. It can include the following:

Pronouns

We	Our	My
He	His	Her
She	Your	
They	Their	

Adverbs

Suddenly	Once	Away
Slowly	Soon	Not
First	Never	Always
Finally	Only	Sometimes

Prepositions

In	Out	Into
On	Beyond	Up
Over	From	By
Under	To	Below

Another good exercise is to have a student write a series of questions and answers.

The next step in improving sentence structure is to teach compound, complex, and run-on sentences. This is best done with some knowledge of grammar.

GRAMMAR

Grammar is important, for the college-bound student. Unfortunately, not only is the student likely to be worried about the task, but many teachers are uncertain when it comes to the more sophisticated and, actually, useful aspects of the subject. I tell students, "The bad thing about learning grammar is that you have to learn some useless material before you get to the useful stuff; knowing the parts of speech comes first, but it will not make you a better writer. But the good thing about it is that it is limited—not like math or history which goes on *forever*. You can learn all the useful grammar in a few months."

Begin with the parts of speech: noun, article, pronoun, adjective, verb, adverb, conjunction, interjection, and preposition, in that order. Any grammar book will do but Treanor's *Grammar* Books I and II and Riddlesbarger and Stillwagon's *Easy English Exercises** are the best I have found because they provide sufficient examples and exercises. Keep the material simple, and press on.

Establish the habit of drawing arrows from adjectives to the nouns they modify and from adverbs to verbs, and of placing parentheses around prepositional phrases. This procedure is simpler than diagramming and almost as effective.

The black cat walked slowly (under the ladder.)

As each part of speech is introduced, assign practice sentences to reinforce the new concept. Develop lists that involve adjectives, adverbs, and later, prepositions. Write a phrase with ten different adjectives. For instance.

the sharp knife

the blunt knife

the long knife

Then vary the noun:

the sharp knife

the sharp stone

the sharp remark

Do the same with adverbs:

he spoke rapidly

he spoke quietly

he spoke firmly

or

he spoke rapidly

he drives rapidly

he climbed rapidly

* See the Selected Bibliography.

Later, try the exercise with prepositional phrases:

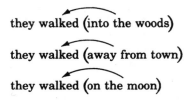

they walked (into the woods)

they walked (away from town)

they walked (on the moon)

or

they walked (into the woods)

they ran (into the woods)

they drove (into the woods)

Verbs are troublesome and are probably best learned by practicing their conjugations. This is a rather old-fashioned exercise, but a useful one. Prepare worksheets with the pronouns in place, initially for just three tenses. (See Sample Worksheet 7.) Assign two of these daily—one regular verb, such as *talk, sail, like,* or *repeat,* which adds *-ed* to the past tense, and one irregular, such as *speak, take, go,* or *do.* Once these three tenses have been mastered, add the three perfect tenses. (See Sample Worksheet 8.) Another useful drill is to have students conjugate a verb, regular or irregular, in a single person.

Tense	Regular
Present	I practice
Past	I practiced
Future	I will practice
Perfect	I have practiced
Past Perfect	I had practiced
Future Perfect	I will have practiced

Tense	Irregular
Present	He teaches
Past	He taught
Future	He will teach
Perfect	He has taught
Past Perfect	He had taught
Future Perfect	He will have taught

Ever since General MacArthur said, "I shall return" when he meant "I will return," the distinction between *shall* and *will* has become purely academic and may not be worth troubling with—simply teach *will* for the future tenses. After all, the goal of this exercise is *not* to make a grammarian out of the dyslexic student, but to improve his ability to construct good sentences.

As soon as the parts of speech have been more or less mastered, begin work with clauses. A clause is a group of words containing a noun or pronoun used as subject, and a verb. A main clause can stand alone: it is a sentence. A subordinate clause is not a sentence and cannot stand alone. It begins with a word called a subordinating conjunction. Write this list of subordinating conjunctions on a five-by-seven-inch card or on the outside cover of a grammar book— in some handy place for ready reference.

Subordinating conjunctions

when	as	so that
whenever	as if	where
before	as soon as	wherever
after	because	though
until	if	although
till	while	even if
as though	since	unless
that	how	in order that

Later add *than* and *why,* which pose special problems, and perhaps even *whence* and *whither.* The student should practice writing subordinate clauses. Since a subordinate clause is not a sentence, but a fragment, it should not be capitalized or followed by a period. The following are examples of subordinate clauses:

whenever I hear the national anthem
although he did not expect to win
before Edison invented the light bulb

A compound sentence consists of two main clauses joined by *and, but, or, nor, for, yet* (preceded by a comma), or by a semicolon. Examples of compound sentences follow:

, and	The snow continued for a week, **and** we were running out of food.
, but	We had lost several battles, **but** our troops were not discouraged.
, or	We can go out to dinner now, **or** we can make the early movie and eat later.
, nor	Paul cannot ski the expert slopes, **nor** can he manage the intermediate runs safely.
, for	The men had given up hope, **for** the boat was leaking badly.
, yet	We left the heat on, **yet** the pipes froze.
;	The race had started; no further bets were possible.

Avoid sentences in which both clauses have the same subject as they are usually best written as simple sentences with a compound verb. "I left home early in the morning, and I caught the first bus into town" is better expressed as "I left home early in the morning and caught the first bus into town." Students can now begin to use their spelling words in compound sentences.

Sample Worksheet 7.

Verb _____

Present (today)	Past (yesterday)	Future (tomorrow)
I _____	I _____	I _____
You _____	You _____	You _____
He/She/It _____	He/She/It _____	He/She/It _____
We _____	We _____	We _____
You _____	You _____	You _____
They _____	They _____	They _____

Verb _____

Present (today)	Past (yesterday)	Future (tomorrow)
I _____	I _____	I _____
You _____	You _____	You _____
He/She/It _____	He/She/It _____	He/She/It _____
We _____	We _____	We _____
You _____	You _____	You _____
They _____	They _____	They _____

A compound sentence with no semicolon or coordinating conjunction is a run-on sentence. It need not be long to be faulty. Make the writing of five or ten run-on sentences a part of the assignment. Once a student knows their structure—two main clauses with nothing to separate them, and a comma is not enough—he will be in a position to identify them quickly and to eliminate them from his own writing.

Here are some student-written examples of run-on sentences.

1. Charlie walked down the hall he was headed for their trap.
2. The chair moved mysteriously, there were no doubts in my mind it was the work of a ghost.
3. Amber Sunshine began her routines, they had not changed for sixty years.
4. I walked into the room, the welcoming committee was very helpful.
5. The teacher was trying to help him he doodled and daydreamed.

Various ways of correcting the sentences can be discussed. The student must be taught that a comma does not fix a run-on sentence. A period or a semicolon will, although the former may result in too many short sentences, and the latter does

Sample Worksheet 8.

Verb _____

Present	Past	Future
I _____	I _____	I _____
You _____	You _____	You _____
He/She/It _____	He/She/It _____	He/She/It _____
We _____	We _____	We _____
You _____	You _____	You _____
They _____	They _____	They _____

Present Perfect (have/has)	Past Perfect (had)	Future Perfect (will have)
I _____	I _____	I _____
You _____	You _____	You _____
He/She/It _____	He/She/It _____	He/She/It _____
We _____	We _____	We _____
You _____	You _____	You _____
They _____	They _____	They _____

not always make sense. Another possibility is the addition of a coordinating conjunction *(and, but, or, nor, for, yet)* preceded by a comma. Often one clause can be made into a subordinate clause by the addition of a relative pronoun or a subordinating conjunction. For the more sophisticated, reducing one element to a verbal may be the most elegant solution.

Even before he has mastered grammar, he can imitate sentence structure and work from a sheet such as Sample Worksheet 9.

Complex sentences, one main clause and one subordinate clause, can be introduced next. Again, at first it may be useful to prepare a sheet with a model pattern such as Sample Worksheet 10. Note that the comma is used or omitted depending on the order of the clauses. For example:

You will be punished if you are late.

Sample Worksheet 9.

Compound Sentence Pattern

noun + verb + details, <u>and</u> noun + verb + details

The horse trotted down the lane, and the owner came running after him.

1. _____

2. _____

3. _____

4. _____

5. _____

noun + verb + details ; noun + verb + details

In 1912 he married; two years later his first son was born.

1. _____

2. _____

3. _____

4. _____

5. _____

---

but

    If you are late, you will be punished.

The list of subordinating conjunctions should be kept handy.

    By now the student will be ready to embark on paragraph writing if he has not done so already. The more detailed study of clauses and verbals are topics that can be taken up later. In the case of the adult or the student who is not planning on college, the section on advanced grammar can be omitted altogether.

ADVANCED GRAMMAR

    First teach the various kinds of subordinate clauses: adjective, adverb, and noun. Begin with adjective clauses.

Sample Worksheet 10.

Complex Sentence Pattern

noun + verb + details + <u>because</u> + noun + verb + details

<u>Because</u> gives a reason.

We were all late that day because my alarm clock had failed to go off.

1. _____

2. _____

3. _____

4. _____

5. _____

<u>when</u> + noun + verb + details, noun + verb + details

<u>When</u> gives a time.

When she applied for the job, she knew the work would be challenging.

1. _____

2. _____

3. _____

4. _____

5. _____

Adjective Clauses

1. An adjective clause describes a noun or pronoun.
2. It usually begins with a relative pronoun—*who, whose, whom, that, which,* or *what.* Students should memorize this list. Compounds such as *whoever* and *whatsoever* can be postponed.
3. It *can be ditched* (i.e., omitted, leaving sentence structure intact). Students should form the habit of placing parentheses around this modifying element to mark its expendable nature, and of drawing an arrow.

Examples:

Sally, (who always drives recklessly,) had an accident last week.

My youngest brother, (who lives in England,) is coming for a visit.

Bruce Jenner, (who won the 1976 decathlon,) is a famous dyslexic.

The book (that I lost last week) has been returned.

Water (that is polluted) is not fit to drink.

The distinction between restrictive and non-restrictive clauses should be taught:

*non*restrictive—commas

restrictive—*no* commas

In the examples above, the first three clauses are nonrestrictive, the last two, restrictive. For instance, the adjective clause in the first sentence does not change (or restrict) the meaning of *Sally*. In the last sentence, however, it is not *all* water that is unfit to drink, but only polluted water.

Adverb Clauses

1. An adverb clause begins with a subordinating conjunction.
2. It modifies a verb and tells how, when, where, why, under what conditions, and to what extent.
3. Like the adjective clause, it can be ditched. Teach students to mark it off by using arrows and parentheses.

How

He looked (as if he were going to throw up.)

They do not study for hours (as we do.)

When

(After she finished talking,) the speaker sat down.

You may leave (when you have finished the exercise.)

Where

Free at last, he sailed his boat (wherever he wanted to go.)

(Where water rises to the surface,) an oasis is formed.

Why

He had difficulty keeping a job (because he was unwilling to work eight hours a day.)

(Since my alarm clock failed to go off,) I missed the wedding altogether.

Under what conditions

(Unless you hurry,) you will miss the plane.

(If that skier does not watch out,) she will fall on that patch of ice.

They went swimming on the beach (although they had been warned about the dangerous surf.)

Postpone adverb clauses and adverbs that modify adjectives and adverbs. This includes *to what extent*. Examples:

He ran so fast (that he fell.)

The slope is so steep (that even goats could not climb it.)

By way of review, it is worth showing students that a noun can be modified in three ways:

the book

the (red) book—by an adjective

the book (with the torn cover)—by a phrase

the book (that I lost)—by a clause

A verb can be similarly modified.

he skied

he skied (fast)—by an adverb

he skied (down the hill)—by a phrase

he skied (because he loved it) (whenever he could)—by a clause

Stress the difference between *paratax*, ideas expressed in simple parallel form, and *syntax*, ideas connected in more sophisticated fashion.

Noun Clauses

The third kind of clause, the noun clause, is more difficult because it requires some background in noun usage. Before beginning noun clauses, go back and teach, or make sure students understand, the various uses of the noun.

- Subject—usually comes first in a sentence
- Direct object—substitute a form of *murder* for the verb and the object becomes the *dead object*. For example: They bought the house on the corner. They murdered the house on the corner. Peter watched the men cutting down the tree. Peter murdered the men . . . . *House* and *men* are dead objects.
- Object of preposition—at the end of a prepositional phrase
- Indirect object—used with verbs meaning "show," "tell," and "give"
- Predicate noun—subject = predicate noun
- Appositive—repeats the subject with no verb between
- Indirect object and appositive can be postponed.

A useful exercise is to give students a noun to use in various ways. For example:

Subject—The <u>ducks</u> are nesting on the pond.
Direct object—We sold our <u>ducks</u>.
Object of preposition—The man came for the <u>ducks</u>.
Indirect object—We fed the <u>ducks</u> bread.
Predicate noun—Those birds flying high are <u>ducks</u>.
Appositive—Those birds, <u>ducks</u>, have been attacked by a mysterious disease.

1. A noun clause begins with a subordinating conjunction or a relative pronoun.
2. It can do anything a noun can do.
3. It takes the place of a noun and cannot be ditched.

Subject:
Noun—My <u>ambition</u> is to travel to the moon.
Noun clause—<u>What I want</u> is to travel to the moon.
Direct Object:
Noun—He always gets a new <u>car</u>.
Noun clause—He always gets <u>what he wants</u>.
Indirect object:
Noun—Give the <u>librarian</u> this book.
Noun clause—Give <u>whoever is in the library</u> this book.
Predicate nominative:
Noun—This book is a <u>classic</u>.
Noun clause—This book is <u>what I want</u>.

Object of preposition:
Noun—This trophy is for <u>Joanna</u>.
Noun clause—This trophy is for <u>whoever runs fastest</u>.
Appositive:
Noun—His story, <u>an adventure</u>, was turned into a novel.
Noun clause—His story, <u>how he was chased by the tiger</u>, was turned into a novel.

When they are learning the three kinds of subordinate clauses, students should be taught first to identify them by using parentheses and arrows and then to compose sentences illustrating the various usages. Since most grammar books do not contain enough practice exercises, several should be used. To the Treanor books and the *Easy English Exercises*, add the *English Review* series by Earl Wood.* Never lose sight of the goal of grammar—to improve writing skill. The subject itself has no intrinsic value for the dyslexic who is unlikely to study foreign languages.

Verbals

Verbals are the last element of use to students and should not be tackled until clauses have been mastered. A verbal is a combination of a verb and some other element. There are three kinds of verbals: participles, gerunds, and infinitives. All of them can be used alone or expanded into phrases.

Participles

1. Participles are adjectives.
2. They modify nouns or pronouns.
3. They can be ditched.
4. They can be expanded.
   running
   running fast
   running fast through the woods
   running fast through the woods in the dark

The phrases are usually set off by commas.

(<u>Running down the hill,</u>) Jill slipped and fell.

(<u>Barking</u>) dogs and (<u>yowling</u>) cats kept me up all night.

It is hard to walk with a (<u>broken</u>) leg.

(<u>Having walked all day,</u>) we went to bed early.

The tree, (<u>having been damaged by the storm,</u>) had to be removed to make the road safe.

*See the Selected Bibliography.

Gerunds

1. The gerund is a verbal noun ending in *ing*.
2. It takes the place of a noun and does all the things a noun can do.
3. It cannot be ditched.

Examples:

Subject—<u>Skiing</u> is fun.

Direct object—He enjoys <u>skiing</u>.

Object of preposition—He lives for <u>skiing</u>.

Indirect object—He gives his <u>skiing</u> a lot of care.

Predicate noun—His favorite sport is <u>skiing</u>.

Appositive—His favorite sport, <u>skiing</u>, was dangerous.

A gerund can be expanded:

driving
driving fast
driving into town at night
driving his new car

A gerund can have its own subject, always in the possessive case.

I object to <u>your</u> chewing gum in class.

John's parents are afraid of <u>his</u> driving at night.

<u>Carol's</u> passing that exam was a triumph.

The Infinitive

The last kind of verbal, the infinitive, *to* plus a verb, is easy to identify, but its usage is difficult to detect since it can be used as an adjective, adverb, or noun (in all uses). Infinitives are not used as objects of prepositions or as indirect objects.

Adjectival:

He needs a book (to read.)

She bought bulbs (to plant in her garden.)

The prince had many servants (to obey his commands.)

They had to abandon their plan (to sail around the world.)

Paula said, "I wish I had a machine (to do my homework.")

Adverbial:

She longs (to travel.)

Caesar came (to conquer Britain.)

They went out (to get some pizza.)

The bank agreed (to lend us the money for the car.)

Susan stayed (to lure the dog into the house.)

Noun:

Subject—<u>To succeed</u> is my aim.

Direct object—Peter wants <u>to succeed</u>.

Predicate nominative—Her aim is <u>to succeed</u>.

Appositive—His ambition, <u>to succeed</u>, has become an obsession.

The study of verbals brings us to the end of formal grammar. However, there are many aspects of what is usually termed syntax, or usage, that are well worth explaining. They include such niceties as the distinction between *and* and *but*, the use of *different from* (instead of *different to* or *than*), the correct placement of modifiers, and the subtleties of pronoun case. These should be taught as the need arises.

The best way of teaching grammar is by having students write single sentences. The dyslexic student will not learn grammar from a series of workbook exercises, nor from looking at the marks a teacher has put on his paper. But writing simple, compound, and complex sentences and, perhaps, learning to use verbals can vastly improve his writing. Doing this preliminary work will enable him to move on to paragraphs with confidence.

4. The Paragraph

PRELIMINARY EXERCISES

The most common complaint subject-matter teachers have about the writing of their students is that their essays lack sufficient supporting data. Planning a paragraph is an exercise in logical thinking. Some of the requisite skills are best developed through the use of pre–paragraph writing activities that require the student to create first lists, then sentences, in support of a given topic. Work on paragraph writing need not be postponed until the material in Chapter 3 has been completed.

From the very beginning of the program, the student should be writing lists of all sorts. Writing a list, besides being fun, is a way of generating ideas, of unleashing the innate creativity of the dyslexic. Like sentence writing, it is a nonthreatening activity. Essentially, a list is a group of similar things or ideas, and the activity provides practice with the sophisticated thinking that depends on perceiving these similarities. A student who has practiced writing lists freely will not have trouble generating appropriate supporting topics when it comes to paragraphs and compositions.

A list of fifteen items seems to be the right length, but, with an individual student the list can be extended to twenty or limited to ten. Needless to say, spelling should be ignored. If a student seems to be more than usually inhibited, use oral exercises—student and teacher contributing in turn. Sometimes such a game can fill a couple of minutes left at the end of a period or provide a moment of relaxation during a session. Many of these lists can encourage a student to exercise his imagination, ingenuity, or humor—several lend themselves readily to subdivision. The following have proved successful, but the best topics are probably those designed for the individual student, or worked out by pupil and teacher in collaboration. The original inspiration for this activity came from the *Book of Lists*.* Have fun with it, and make it fun for your students.

Things in your room	Kinds of cereal
T.V. stars	Junk/health foods
T.V. programs	Rock groups
Trees	T-shirt slogans
Soft drinks	Kinds of tools
Kinds of cars	Zoo animals
Sweet things to eat	Holidays
Uses of a brick	Uses of a match
Weapons	Cutting tools
Girls' names	Boys' names
Signs of being sick	Ways of getting exercise
Blue things	Red things
Hard things	Soft things
Insects	Paper objects
Musical instruments	Camping gear
Stable equipment	Kinds of weather
Kinds of reptiles	Parts of a car
Animals with fur	Fast food restaurants
Food I like/hate	Things people collect
Parts of a motorcycle	Colors
Articles of clothing	Kinds of candy
Board games	Team sports
Famous men	Famous women
Things I like to do	Parts of a boat
Kinds of stores	Pet peeves
April Fool tricks	Kinds of vegetables
Kinds of fruit	Flowers
Worries	Kinds of illnesses
Football players	Basketball teams
Movies	Magazines
Man-made objects	Compound words
Homonyms	Things that need oil
Things that need bulbs	Clothing labels
Relatives you can have	T.V. commercials
Indoor hobbies	Winter sports
Kinds of birds	Halloween costumes
Colleges	Excuses for being late
Professions	Common last names
Fabrics	Herbs and spices
Proverbs	Mottos

*David Wallechinsky and Irving Wallace, *Book of Lists* (New York: William Morrow & Co., 1977).

Signs of winter/spring/summer/fall
Things that glow in the dark
Things that you could have in your pocket
Things to put in sandwiches
Excuses for not doing assignments
Words that begin with *st*
Things that run on batteries
Word pairs (cup and saucer, lost and found)
Things in a medicine cabinet
Things to say to a girl/boy you'd like to date
Articles of ski clothing and equipment
Tapes you would like to own
Things that cost under a dollar
Current political issues
Advantages of city life
Reasons for failing a course
Dangerous driving habits
Things you could bet on
Ways of saving money

The next pre–paragraph writing exercise is similar to lists. It requires the student to generate three or more supporting statements, given a topic sentence. The paper should be designed so that the student writes separate sentences, beginning each on a new line. (See Sample Worksheet 11.)

After a few days, go back over the skeleton paragraphs and work out a good concluding sentence for each. The paragraph on table manners might end with, "I avoid sitting next to him at meals" or "His parents do not seem to have taught him anything." You now have five sentences, the basis for a paragraph, and, ultimately, for a five-paragraph essay.

The next step to introduce is that of composing topic sentences. This is a more sophisticated task that involves a higher level of abstract thinking. At first, the assignment should be to formulate a topic sentence and, perhaps, a concluding sentence to fit a series of supporting sentences. The teacher should prepare exercises similar to Sample Worksheet 12. After some practice, the student will be ready to write a five-sentence paragraph from a given topic. Practice this for a few days.

Next, say to your student, "Suppose you wanted to give more information about each support—to write several sentences instead of just one. Then you would need some way of keeping your ideas apart. Here are some useful words to use: *first, next* or *then,* and *last* or *finally*." Write your topic sentence. Use the word *first* and tell all about your first supporting idea. Then use *next* or *then* and talk about your second support. Then use *finally* or *last* and write about your third point."

Illustrated next is what Emily wrote after only three weeks of tutoring one summer. In the fourth grade of a competitive private school she had been having trouble writing more than three of four sentences on any subject. Given the instructions above, she responded immediately.

Christmas is my favorite holiday for several reasons. First is I get to see my cousin. I like seeing my cousin Sarah. We always find things to do like playing in the snow. Sometimes we go out to the bay where my aunt lives. We play on the trails out there. Next is giving and getting presents. I like giving presents because it makes me feel happy. The only problem is that I don't always have enough money. I like getting presents because I have new things to do. I like getting stuffed animals and books. I hate getting clothes. Last is that there is snow. I love the snow. I have snowball fights. Some kids made a sledslide out of snow for my sister's birthday. I think snow is a lot of fun but then there is a time when it's not that is when I get cold. I sure do like Christmas.*

Transition words are best introduced a few at a time in this informal fashion. As they are introduced, they should be written down for ready reference—perhaps on the inside cover of the student's notebook.

At this stage introduce *tandem writing,* an exercise in which student and teacher write simultaneously. Writing can be a lonely process and one that students tend to avoid. Given a list of assignments, it is often the writing assignment that will be ignored. Writing in class with a teacher is helpful. In tandem writing the teacher is writing too, not merely sitting and watching, or correcting papers. In partnership with the student, agree on a topic and a topic sentence. Teacher and student can take turns choosing. Students take great pleasure in challenging me with topics such as *computers* or *rock music,* about which I know nothing. But the teacher should take pains to choose something about which a student knows something. Agree on an approximate length— "Let's try to write a page this time"—and start together. The objective is not to outwrite the student, but to produce a structured paragraph within ten minutes or so. Then student and teacher exchange papers, read one another's, and, perhaps, enter into a discussion about whatever seems relevant. It is important to make the exercise fun. In a class, students can work in pairs. Three short paragraphs I wrote with a student follow on page 36.

*The original contained six spelling errors, which have been corrected.

Write three supporting statements for each topic sentence.

Some animals are useful to man.

1. _____
2. _____
3. _____

My room was untidy.

1. _____
2. _____
3. _____

You can do many things while you wait at an airport.

1. _____
2. _____
3. _____

Hitchhiking is dangerous.

1. _____
2. _____
3. _____

His table manners are terrible.

1. _____
2. _____
3. _____

Sample Worksheet 12.

Write a topic sentence and a concluding sentence for each group of supporting sentences.

T.S. _____

1. I was late for school.
2. My books fell in the mud.
3. When I went to hand in my math homework, I discovered it was gone.

C.S. _____

T.S. _____

1. My neighbor gave me $5.00 for mowing the lawn.
2. I earned $10.00 washing and waxing a car.
3. My father paid me $5.00 for cleaning out the garage.

C.S. _____

T.S. _____

1. John didn't hand in his homework for several weeks.
2. He failed two of the three quizzes.
3. He never completed his science project.

C.S. _____

T.S. _____

1. You'll never see me walk under a ladder.
2. I won't go anywhere without my four-leaf clover.
3. Black cats make me go in the opposite direction.

C.S. _____

T.S. _____

1. I woke up with a sore throat.
2. I sneezed several times at breakfast.
3. My nose and eyes are watering.

C.S. _____

Paragraph 1—Student:

Getting Something for Nothing

I usually never win anything. For the past two years I have been playing bingo after school. I was the kind of guy who may come in second three or four times in a row. I got four in a row within the first seven calls. I havent a figured out the math of it, but I'de bet noones ever done that before.

Paragraph 1—Me:

Getting Something for Nothing

I never win anything. While a million dollars would be great, I never even bother to buy a lottery ticket. At Ames Plaza, the supermarket gives away some sort of stamps. I tell the clerk to keep them. If I have to buy a raffle ticket, I throw it away. The only things I get free are the shells I find on the beach.

Paragraph 2—Student:

Many things can go wrong with a car. A car that may cost six thousand dollars has many gadgets in it. It is possible that one of the gadgets may not work well or become inoperative after some use. The car will show signs of something being wrong. It this is not correctly analized, the engine may have to be taken apart. This is very bad for the engine and the car may not run as well because of origionaly one little fault.

Paragraph 2—Me:

Many things can go wrong with a car. Even in these days of radial tires, a flat is not uncommon. Then, the electrical system can malfunction, leaving the driver without lights or starter. Worst of all, the brakes can fail. The safety conscious driver will have his vehicle checked regularly by a competent mechanic.

Paragraph 3—Student:

He was neatly dressed. First his tie matched his jaket and was perfectly notted. Also, his shoes were freshly shined. Finally the creases in his black pants were bold. He looked as if he might be dinning at the Whitehouse.

Paragraph 3—Me:

He was neatly dressed. His striped shirt was crisply ironed. His tweed jacket fitted him well. His tie, carefully selected to harmonize with his jacket and shirt, was neatly tied. I would hire him on the spot for any job that involved impressing the public.

TYPES OF PARAGRAPHS

The next step is to teach the various types of paragraphs, beginning with the simplest and proceeding to the more complex. In order, they are as follows:

1. Example	2. Process
3. Classification	4. Reason
5. Definition	6. Comparison and contrast
7. Description	8. Narration

Introduce these one at a time, and do not go on to the next until the student has written a couple of good paragraphs of each kind. In general, when working with a dyslexic student, avoid having him recopy. Copying is a singularly tiresome task for the dyslexic—it involves exactly that sort of eye-hand coordination that he finds most difficult. In many instances, the recopying process leads to additional errors, not to mention an entrenched dislike of all writing tasks. It is far better to have a student write another paragraph on a different topic. In selecting topics, proceed from the simple and familiar to the more abstract and academic. Continue to introduce new transition words as needed. Learning to formulate good topic sentences will have to be an ongoing process. Introduce the student to this useful list.

examples of	similarities between
results of	differences between
causes of	kinds of
reasons for	types of
advantages of	way(s) of
disadvantages of	

The most useful kind of outline is the scratch outline. The student should be encouraged to jot down a list of possible supporting ideas, to select those he wants to use, and to decide on their best order. The elaborate outline, using correct signs of logical rank and writing full sentences, or carefully worded parallel topics, comes later; it is, in practice, less useful. But teach a student to make a quick scratch outline and he will do so even under the stress of an examination.

Order is important. Wherever possible, ideas should be arranged either in chronological order, first to last, *or* in order of importance, least important to most important.

Begin to teach the student to devise appropriate titles for his paragraphs so that this habit will be established by the time he begins full-length essays.

The Example Paragraph

Possible Topics

Dangerous Animals	Ways of Saving Money
Useful Inventions	Common Superstitions
Interesting Places to Visit	Interesting Jobs
Things I Could Do Without	Kinds of Diets
People I Admire	Hobbies
Things That Annoy Me	Popular Magazines
Ways of Earning Money	Favorite Movies

The example paragraph is the easiest to develop. Specific, concrete, carefully selected examples are important to all good writing.

Useful Transitions

for example	for instance
in particular	another example
the last example	

The Process Paragraph

Possible Topics

How to Change a Tire	How to Develop a Film
How to Do Laundry	How to Start a Hobby
How to Wash Dishes	How to Get Rid of Mice
How to Cure a Cold	How to Annoy a Teacher
My Favorite Sandwich	Caring for House Plants
Grooming a Horse	How to Mend Something
How to Lose/Gain Weight	How to Cook Something

The process paragraph is best written in time order. The paragraph may have to begin by describing what material to collect before the process begins. Then it will go on to describe the many different steps involved in the process. Point of view must be consistent—this is a good place to teach students that writing cannot change from *I* to *you* in midstream.

Useful Transitions

first, second, third	to begin with
then	at this point
next	when
also	at last
after	last
moreover	finally
furthermore	afterwards
before	

The Classification Paragraph

Possible Topics

Kinds of Snakes	Dogs
Types of Headgear	T.V. Programs
Kinds of Games	Rock Bands
Kinds of Stores	Jobs
Cars	Sports
Tools	Fish
Magazines	T.V. Commercials

The categories should be few in number, perhaps two or three, and must include everything in the group. Making a list might be an initial step in deciding on what basis to classify. Once the basis of classification has been established (e.g., poisonous/nonpoisonous snakes), several examples of each can be selected for inclusion in the paragraph.

Useful Transitions

the first/the second/the third
one kind/another kind
one type of/another type of
the best/worst type/kind
the last type/kind

The Reason Paragraph

Possible Topics

Why I Enjoy Hiking
Why Traveling Is Fun
Why I Stopped Smoking
Why the Drinking Age Should Be 21
Why I Want to Attend College
Why I Enjoy/Avoid Parties
Why People Cheat
The Benefits of Jogging
Why I Keep My Hair Long/Short
Why I Watch T.V.
Why Pollution Must Be Stopped
Why Fast-Food Restaurants Are Popular
Why _____ Won the Election
Why _____ Went Out of Business
Advantages of Working for Oneself
The Benefits of Weight Lifting
Why I Plan to Vote for _____
Why I Need to Earn Money
Why People Lie
_____ Should Be Abolished

Each reason should be followed by a set of descriptive details and, perhaps, examples. Reasons are best placed in climactic order, least to most important. Avoid sentences starting with *because* and especially the phrase, *the reason is because*.

Useful Transitions

one reason
another reason
the first/second/third reason
the final reason
the last reason
the most important reason
therefore
as a result
consequently

The Definition Paragraph

Possible Topics

Freedom	A Liberated Woman
Peace	Jazz
Cruelty	Rock Music
Home	Selfishness
"Cool"	Homesickness
A Redneck	Magic
Happiness	A Hippie
Democracy	Spring
Prejudice	Anger
A Hero	A Friend

There are many ways of writing a definition. Do not permit your student to begin with Webster, but teach him to define by example, by synonyms, by stating what something is not, or by explaining the distinction between similar terms, or, for the imaginative, by analogy.

The Comparison and Contrast Paragraph

Possible Topics

Two Restaurants	Two Schools
BMX Bicycle versus 10-Speed	Two Jobs
Teenagers versus Children	Two Cars
Two Musical Instruments	Two Sports
Flying versus Traveling by Bus	Two Magazines
Two Grocery Stores	Two Teachers
Country Life versus City Life	Two Cities
Cats versus Dogs as Pets	Two States
Sailboats versus Motorboats	Two Parks
Two Television Commercials	Two Video Games

If the topic is a short one, a paragraph about each will suffice, but if the subject to be treated is more extensive, each aspect must be treated separately.

Jogging versus Weight Lifting

I. Equipment needed
   A. Jogging
   B. Weight lifting
II. Time required
   A. Jogging
   B. Weight lifting
III. Problems
   A. Jogging
   B. Weight lifting
IV. Benefits
   A. Jogging
   B. Weight lifting

Note that the objects compared must always be mentioned in the same order. *Compare* usually means both "compare and contrast," but the student should understand the distinction.

Useful Transitions

Comparing	*Contrasting*
both	by contrast
also	on the other hand
too	unlike
have in common	instead of
share the same	but
another	another difference

The Descriptive Paragraph

Possible Topics

The Beach in Summer	My Home
My Street	A Souvenir
My Favorite Place	A Walk in the Rain
A Ski Slope	A Person
A Flea Market	A Haunted House
A Garage Sale	A Castle
A Drug Store	An Arcade
One of My Childhood Possessions	

Description can be precise and objective or impressionistic. In expository writing the purpose must be kept in mind. Why is the writer describing this scene? Make lists of adjectives and of phrases that will convey the sounds, sights, and smells of the scene. Many dyslexics have a real knack for poetic description.

The Narrative Paragraph

Possible Topics

My First Job
My First Pet
An Event That Changed Me
A Frustrating Experience
A Childhood Memory
An Action I've Always Regretted
My First Car Accident
How Our Team Won
The Day I Got Lost
How I Learned to Skate
Snowbound
A Trip
The Most Dangerous Thing I've Done
How I Learned about Poverty
Getting My Driver's License

Students will write best about what they have experienced, and their best writing will be based on reality. The beginner should stick to time order, but the more advanced student can be taught to begin just before the climax and to fill in the earlier events later. The use of dialogue to make writing more vivid and of descriptive detail are other topics to pursue. Again, if this is to be expository writing, some purpose must be kept in mind.

DEVELOPING TOPIC SENTENCES

Once students have learned the various types of paragraphs, it is worth spending some time on the development of good topic sentences. In this connection, two exercises have proved useful. The first requires the student to label a series of topic sentences according to the type of paragraph they best fit. (See Sample Worksheets 13 and 14.)

The second exercise involves writing a topic sentence of each type, given a general topic such as poverty, rock music, current political problems, computers, or school. (See Sample Worksheet 15.) Topic sentences are crucial because they determine the type of paragraph as well as place limits on what it can contain.

One by-product of these writing exercises is improved reading comprehension. The student who has practiced writing topic sentences and various kinds of paragraphs will be quicker to detect the structure in his textbooks and better at separating main ideas from their supports. Outlining from the text will also be easier for him to master.

Sample Worksheet 13.

Topic Sentence Drill 1

Some ways to develop paragraphs:

A. Explain a *process* 　　　　E. Describe a *scene*

B. Supply *reasons* 　　　　　F. *Compare* and *contrast*

C. Provide *examples* 　　　　G. *Define* a term

D. Relate an *event* 　　　　　H. Divide and *classify*

Match the following topic sentences with the appropriate type of paragraph development.

_____ There are a number of reasons for our high crime rate.

_____ The most embarrassing moment of my life occurred last week.

_____ I would rather live in the country than in the city.

_____ A friend is the one who takes the time when there isn't any.

_____ Childhood can be divided into three developmental stages.

_____ You will be sure to fail a test if you follow a series of simple steps.

_____ I felt a warm rush of air as I entered the cozy living room.

_____ Seeds can be dispersed in four different ways.

_____ My first day as a busboy was one I'll never forget.

_____ My father is a patient man.

_____ Several factors led to my recent driving accident.

_____ To change a tire, you should follow a series of steps.

_____ I have driven both an economy car and a luxury car, and there are many differences between the two.

SELECTING TOPICS

For students to become confident writers they need to begin by writing about the familiar. The painter Constable in writing about his subject matter, the Suffolk countryside, said: "But the sound of water excaping from Mill dams . . . willow, old rotten banks, slimy posts, and brickwork. I love such things . . . As long as I do paint I shall never cease to paint such places." Writing begins with the personal and the familiar.

Hemingway knew about fishing, big game hunting, and war, and Steinbeck, about the Salinas Valley, because they had lived these things. Students who can describe their own experiences, who can write vividly about familiar things, and who have established a successful writing habit will not have difficulty in dealing with subject-matter courses. Good writing is simple and direct; the student who finds himself pushed into writing about social studies, science, and literature at too early a stage is likely to develop a pretentious style difficult to eradicate.

Sample Worksheet 14.

Topic Sentence Drill 2

Match the types of paragraphs to the sentences below by writing the appropriate letter before each sentence.

A. Example   D. Reason   G. Description

B. Process   E. Definition   H. Narration

C. Classification   F. Comparison and Contrast

_____ A person can build a strong memory by following two basic steps and using six memory aids.

_____ I did not think my parents would return before midnight.

_____ My bedroom is my favorite place.

_____ Cars can be classified into four groups, according to the image the driver wants to portray.

_____ My sister is a generous person.

_____ Loneliness is being a drop of water with no puddle to fall into.

_____ I prefer the country to the city.

_____ New York is a wonderful place to live.

_____ I refused the invitation for several reasons.

_____ There are several types of downhill skis on the market.

_____ I thought we had enough gas to make it back.

_____ Keeping your houseplants healthy is easy if you follow these simple instructions.

_____ The view from my window is spectacular.

_____ Some plants and animals can survive desert conditions.

Sample Worksheet 15.

Rock Music

Compose a topic sentence that fits each type of paragraph.

Example

T.S. _____

_____

Process

T.S. _____

_____

Classification

T.S. _____

_____

Reason

T.S. _____

_____

Definition

T.S. _____

_____

Comparison and Contrast

T.S. _____

_____

Description

T.S. _____

_____

Narration

T.S. _____

_____

5. The Essay

Once the student has mastered paragraph writing, expanding his ideas into a full-length essay is an easy transition. The pattern is similar. (See Figure 24.)

Proceed from the simple to the complex, introducing essay topics in the same order as you introduced the kinds of paragraphs. Some of the previously written paragraphs can readily be expanded into full-length essays. Begin with these paragraphs and develop similar topics.

In an essay, the topic sentence, called the thesis statement, is the most difficult to write. It must reflect not merely a fact but an attitude or opinion about a fact. For example, "My first job was mowing lawns" is not a satisfactory thesis statement. A better thesis statement is "I learned a lot from my first job, mowing lawns" or "The worst job I ever had was mowing lawns." The statement should be bold and definite: in-my-opinion-I-think-that sentences should be avoided. Presumably the writer thinks or believes what he writes.

In the introductory paragraph the thesis statement should be followed by a concise plan of development, listing the supporting points in order. For example, "La Vista is the best restaurant in town. The food is delicious, the atmosphere peaceful, and the service excellent." In the essay, one paragraph is then devoted to developing each of the three points.

In addition to the thesis statement and the plan of development, the introductory paragraph should ideally contain a lead-in, in the form of some sort of introductory remarks designed to arouse the reader's interest. This part of the introductory paragraph is often difficult to compose. Some writers prefer to add it after the rest of the essay has been finished. It may be useful to work with the student on a whole series of introductory paragraphs without necessarily completing the essays for which they were designed. *Reader's Digest* or other popular magazines are often a good source of material for discussion. Collect samples such as the following to illustrate the most common beginnings.

1. A question
   Have you ever wanted to learn to surf?
   What happens to our taxes?
2. An explanation of why the subject is important to the reader
   Learning to control a car in a skid may help you avert an accident.
   You can save a lot of money by remodeling your basement yourself.

Figure 24.

Paragraph	Essay
Topic sentence	Introductory paragraph including *thesis* statement
1. Supporting sentence	1. Supporting paragraph
2. Supporting sentence	2. Supporting paragraph
3. Supporting sentence	3. Supporting paragraph
Concluding sentence	Concluding paragraph

---

3. A statement the opposite of the point to be developed

Most people believe that all the food you can buy at a supermarket is safe to eat.

Surely there are advantages to communism.

4. A quotation

Polonius said, "Neither a borrower nor a lender be."

According to Oscar Wilde, "There is no sin except stupidity."

5. An incident of some sort

"One evening after work, Jane Myers [not her real name] boarded a crowded Manhattan bus, her purse slung over her shoulder by its strap. When she transferred to another bus, she found her pocketbook open and the wallet gone."*

This is a device often used by professional writers. However, it is not a new one; all the parables in the Bible are examples of the speaker's getting the attention of his audience in this fashion.

Not only should each paragraph begin with a topic sentence but, where possible, all topic sentences should also form a link with the preceding paragraph.

Thesis statement: La Vista is the best restaurant in town.
1. The food is delicious.
2. *Just as impressive as the food* is the beautiful dining room.
3. *In this atmosphere* the waiters move with silent efficiency.

A good concluding paragraph will come more naturally to the student who has practiced writing concluding sentences to paragraphs. If no apt final comment comes to mind and inspiration fails utterly, the concluding paragraph can be a mere repetition of the points covered. Since these will have already been stated in the plan of development, as well as expanded in the supporting paragraphs, this third repetition can

*Richard Wolkomir, "How to Keep Your Wallet Safe," *Reader's Digest*, (December 1984): 51.

fall flat, particularly in a short essay. What is needed is some fresh perspective. Possible conclusions to be considered by the writer include:

1. What the writer has learned

Never again will I try to save money by hitchhiking.

It is hard to make money by growing vegetables.

2. What the reader can learn (i.e., advice)

Do not assume that because a product is cheap, it is the best buy.

People who appear unfriendly may just be shy.

3. An evaluation

Clearly, no small business can afford to be without a computer.

Dairy farming is rapidly becoming a losing proposition.

4. Time

No longer does it take three months to cross the Atlantic.

Thus, child rearing practices have changed considerably during the last thousand years.

5. Space

In Sweden professional boxing is illegal.

In many parts of the world, there is a serious shortage of food.

This method of dealing with essays in a structured fashion—five paragraphs, five kinds of introductions, five kinds of conclusions—is not intended to set limits. Obviously an essay can be developed in many different ways, any thesis statement or topic sentence can have more than three supports, and a piece of writing can have more than five ways of beginning and ending. The purpose of this structure is to form a framework that will enable the writer to get started and to cope confidently with any writing assignment. Nor does the fact that this book is confined to exposition mean that other forms of writing—narration, description, persuasion, and even poetry—should be excluded. However, it is expository writing that is essential to survival in high school and college.

6. Spelling—Some Thoughts

I don't give a damn for a man that can spell a word only one way.—Mark Twain

Most writers, no matter how badly they spell, can read what they have written. Louise Clarke writes:

> I sat down beside Mike and made a jolting discovery. *He knew what he had written.* Furthermore, with him to do the decoding, the answers were correct. I remember "Nloond" particularly. It was in answer to a question on the third line down over to the right of the page. "London," Mike said impatiently.*

Reasonably phonetic spelling, while incorrect, can be read by any teacher. My own favorite misspelling is that of a sixteen-year-old student of mine who wrote *feeonsay*, utterly incorrect, but perfectly comprehensible. But most students come much closer than the examples cited above. So it is that, as much as anything, the problem lies with the stigma attached to poor spelling. There remains the lingering suspicion that laziness or carelessness lies behind the misspelled word—that it is an insult to the reader. "Young man," said his college professor to Charles MacGill, a former student of mine, "See that book. That's a dictionary. All you have to do is memorize it."

Reading can nearly always be remediated to the point at which the student can read up to the level of his intelligence—not necessarily fast, but with excellent comprehension. Spelling is another matter; some dyslexics will not, at least during their school careers, be able to spell beyond a fifth- or sixth-grade level.

There are obvious advantages to starting work with the young child who has not been frustrated by years of school failure; on the other hand, by adolescence maturation has taken place:

visual and auditory discrimination and retention have improved, sequencing difficulties have abated, and reversals are less common. The adolescent has a better chance of learning to spell.

As far as spelling is concerned, dyslexia means that no matter how often a student has seen a word, he cannot reproduce its exact configuration. The visual recall is weak. Three other avenues for spelling are more likely to be successful.

1. *The auditory sense.* English is a Germanic language and most English words are phonetic. The auditory sense can be trained. Auditory discrimination and recall do respond to training provided the language is broken down into its component parts (single sounds) and provided these parts are built into longer sequences gradually and in logical fashion. Training in phonics is always worthwhile.

2. *The kinesthetic sense.* The motor memory is strong. No one who has once learned to swim or to ride a bicycle worries about forgetting these movements.

The kinesthetic sense involves the feeling of movement as the hand writes the word. Grace Fernald taught young children to read and write only by tracing and it worked. However, it is not an efficient method, and had she not been hard of hearing—she used an ear trumpet—she would doubtless have involved phonics in her teaching.

Another less appreciated form of kinesthetic involvement is that of the movement of the speech organs. Naming the letters aloud as one writes, the Orton-Gillingham S.O.S., or Simultaneous Oral Spelling, reinforces language in two ways—through the kinesthetic sense as the student feels the movement of the speech organs and through the auditory sense as he hears the word spelled.

---

*Louise Clarke, *Can't Read, Can't Write, Can't Talk Too Good Either* (New York: Penguin Books, Inc., 1974).

It is important to explain this principle to students, who are less likely to resent being asked to write a word ten times if they understand the exercise as kinesthetic reinforcement—"your hand will teach your brain how to spell it"—rather than some medieval form of punishment.

Good cursive handwriting is a prerequisite for effective kinesthestic reinforcement.

3. *Intelligence.* Much of spelling is logical and involves making the correct choice from two or more possibilities in accordance with rules and generalizations. Learning how to make correct choices can be fun for both teacher and student. Most spelling rules have few exceptions—many have none—and they are well worth teaching. Even more useful is the series of generalizations that deals with correct choice of diphthongs (*ow/ou, oi/oy, au/aw,* etc.) and of long-vowel spellings.

Probably one of the reasons why dyslexics are accused of being careless spellers is that they misspell most readily the common simple words but spell longer words correctly. The trouble is that errors such as *thay, wus, whith, whitch, siad,* and *frome* were learned in the early grades when the perceptual processes were at their least mature, and they have been practiced assiduously ever since. The longer Latin sequences learned later in life stood a better chance of being mastered correctly. Needless to say, the student who has practiced *thay* for ten years or so will have a difficult time eliminating this misspelling which has become entrenched in his kinesthetic memory.

These commonly misspelled words should be placed on three-by-five cards for repeated drill over a long period of time. They should be written ten times each, used in sentences, and dictated until they have been spelled correctly on at least three successive occasions. They should then be reviewed from time to time throughout the year. Words selected from a student's own writings will be of more use than those taken from any standard list. The words in a student's active writing vocabulary are the ones he most needs to know. Only when these common misspellings have been eliminated should a standard list be used.

Words for spelling should be written in felt-tip pen on the unlined side of the card. Grouping similar words is helpful, as is any mnemonic device or picture clue. Keep the words in a box or, more convenient, a small expanding envelope. Words should be marked with a √ for correct, or an X for incorrect each time they are dictated. Make the marks across the top of the card, from left to right. After a word has been spelled correctly on three successive occasions, it can be retired; draw a vertical line after the third √ to indicate this. Thereafter, it can be reviewed periodically. Within the manila envelope or box, words can be grouped as √, √√, √√√, and new or X (to be written). Use a card folded in half to separate each group. It is worth being systematic about these cards.

Sample cards have been reduced.

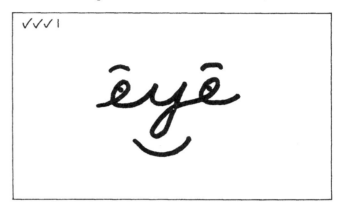

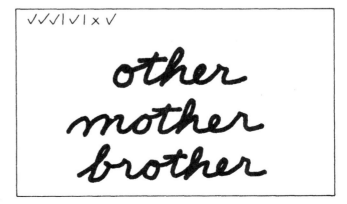

✓ × ✓ ✓

soldier

must die

✓ × × ✓ ✓

coming

come + ing

e rule

A similar system can be developed for vocabulary by writing the word on one side of the card and the definition on the other side. The usual lists, notebooks, and workbooks provide less reinforcement than the dyslexic needs for permanent mastery. Greek and Latin prefixes, helpful for reading as well as for spelling, should also be placed on cards. Memory will always be a problem for the dyslexic, and the three-by-five–card habit is useful throughout high school and college for terminology, dates, names, and formulae.

PHONICS

The manner in which sounds are presented to the adolescent is different from that used in working with younger children. Most adolescents know consonant sounds, or at least a reasonable facsimile thereof; it is the vowels and their combinations that need immediate attention.

Begin with the short vowels in closed syllables.

Short Vowels
a—wax
e—melts
i—in
o—hot
u—sun
y—(same as *i*)

The sentence—wax melts in hot sun—is more useful than a set of isolated key words. In any event, key words should be phased out as soon as possible. It is better to have the student repeat after you:

a is /ă/,
e is /ĕ/,
i is /ĭ/,
o is /ŏ/,
u is /ŭ/.

Say it with him, over and over again until he can do it alone. Never ask a student to "go study your sounds"—this is an in-class activity. Do not include key words; what you are after is a letter-sound association established in the speech organs as kinesthetic memory.

The *e/i* distinction is a difficult one for students raised in the South, who tend to call a dime *tin* cents. As a teaching technique, have the student pronounce /ĕ/ with lips relaxed and /ĭ/ with lips tensed. Another troublesome pair is *o* and *u*. /ŭ/ is produced further back in the mouth, and /ŏ/ is pronounced with rounded lips, especially by the British. Do not despair if these short vowels prove a sticking point; tell your student that they *are* the most difficult sounds in the language. Drill with dictated lists of three-letter nonsense syllables or detached syllables. Having the student stop and tell you the vowel sound *first* may help. Pronounce the sounds in isolation for quick drill. Do not dwell exclusively on short vowels, even for a day; they are tough and will require work over an extended period of time.

Teach three kinds of syllables; often this is a good topic for the first day.

closed	nŏt	ends in a consonant; vowel is short
open	nō	ends in a vowel; vowel is long
silent-*e*	nōtę	ends in a silent *e*; vowel is long

If you find any problems with consonant sounds, clear them up as they occur. For instance, /m/ is pronounced with lips together; /n/ with lips apart; /b/ is made with the lips; /d/ behind the teeth. The sound /f/ is unvoiced, while /v/ is voiced (have the student place his hand on his throat to feel the distinction). Include consonant combinations (digraphs) such as *ch, sh, th, qu* (/kw/) and *x* (/ks/).

Long Vowels*

	Open Syllable	Silent-e Syllable
a	baby	safe
e	secret	these
i	spider	pine
o	pony	home
u	music	mule
y	cyclone	type

A long vowel *says* its name and is easy to discriminate. The exception is *u*, which is often pronounced /o͞o/. In this regard, English is in a state of flux. In tennis, do you say /dūs/ or /do͞os/? Anna Gillingham once told me she was taught to pronounce *flute* as /flūt/. Try it!

Proceed quickly to two-syllable phonetic words such as *in vade, to paz, ni trate,* and *ben zene* and to three-syllable words such as *re fresh ment, ex e cute,* and *in vest ment.* Dividing paper into columns and having a student write each syllable in a separate column will increase his accuracy.

Syllabification is best taught by three simple formulae (V = vowel, C = consonant).

1. VC CV   trumpet
2. V̄CV   tūlip (the division creates an open syllable)
3. V̆CV   căbin (the division creates a closed syllable)

Vowel and consonant combinations are treated as a single unit. Obviously this is an oversimplification, but it is a pragmatic one; we are not training secretaries. Syllabification is better taught with swooping lines than with the usual vertical divisions, which tend to obscure the letters.

Consonants with two sounds are troublesome, especially *c* and *g* because of the sequencing involved.

c	/k/	cat
	/s/	before *e, i, y*
		cent, city, fancy
g	/g/	go
	/j/	before *e, i, y*
		gentle, gin, gym
s	/s/	sit
	/z/	the end of a word or between vowels
		his, nose

Much drill is required here for reading as well as writing.

* Throughout this section, Gillingham key words are used. See the Selected Bibliography.

Next come the following diphthongs and *r*-modified vowels.

oi	boil
oy	boy
ou	out
ow	cow
au	August (an awful pair that
aw	saw needs extra drill)
o͞o	moon
o͝o	book
ar	car
er	her
or	for

Then present a chart of the common long-vowel spellings as follows:

a	a-e	ai	ay
e	e-e	ea	ee
i	i-e	igh	y
o	o-e	oa	ow
u	u-e	ue	ew

These should be memorized as quickly as possible and recited in this form: "Open syllable *a*, *a*-consonant-*e*, *ai*, *ay*."

A sound knowledge of these long-vowel charts is the single most helpful material adolescents can acquire. Many dyslexics, by adolescence, know when a word is wrong. A student who is sure of the range of possibilities, who can take a moment to think and to write them out and consider them, will almost unerringly choose the correct spelling, even when there are several possibilities.

That the vowel alone is used in an open syllable—open-syllable *a, e, i, o,* and *u*—will save a student from such errors as *occaision, toetal,* or *sealect.* In each case the open-syllable spelling is a fairly clear-cut choice and it is only the mid-syllable spelling that varies.

Work with the long-vowel spellings in this order: *a, o, i, e,* and *u.* The instructions in the Gillingham-Stillman manual are useful but should be simplified and adapted, as shown below, since the rare spellings are better postponed altogether. In each case, make a chart with four columns.

Long *a*

a	a-e	ai	ay
baby	safe	sail	play
open syllable	mid-syllable choice		end of word

Lists of words should be dictated for the student to place in the appropriate column. Always, he is asked to give a reason: "open syllable," "end of word," or "mid-syllable and it could be *a-e* or *ai*, but I think it is. . . ." Note that *a-e* is more common than *ai* in the final syllable of a multisyllabic word, e.g., *migrate*, *separate*, *engage*, *brigade*, and *regale*, although *tain* is used in words such as *contain*, *retain*, and *detain*.

The long-*o* spelling follows the same pattern.

Long *o*

o	o-e	oa	ow
pony	home	boat	snow
open syllable	mid-syllable choice		end of word

Again, in the final syllable of a multisyllabic word, *o-e* is more common than *oa*, as in *postpone*, *erode*, and *envelope*.

Long *i*

i	i-e	igh	y
spider	pine	night	my
open syllable	mid-syllable choice		end of word*

The *i* pattern is the same, but *igh* is relatively rare and is usually found in monosyllables ending in *t*, e.g., *light*, *fright*, *flight*, *bright*, and *sight*.

Long *e*

e	e-e	ea	ee
secret	these	eat	feed
open syllable	mid-syl. choice		end of word choice

The *e* pattern is more complex. In the middle of a word, there is a three-way choice, e.g., *mete*, *meat*, or *meet*; but in longer words *e-e* is more likely, hence *complete*, *compete*, *extreme*, *sincere*, and *athlete*. At the end of a word the choice is between *ea* and *ee*, but long words always end in *ee*, e.g., *degree*, *employee*, and *committee*.

In the four long-vowel spellings above, the combinations *ai*, *oa*, *igh*, and *ea* occur for the most part in Anglo-Saxon (short and common) words. The dyslexic student tends to err by overusing these spellings.

Long *u*

u	u-e	ue	ew
music	mule	rescue	few
open syllable	mid-syllable		end of word choice

The long *u* spelling differs in that the choice occurs in the final spelling. Note that *ue* is more common than *ew*.

Until the student is thoroughly familiar with these choices, the other possibilities should be postponed. Wait at least a month before introducing the rare spellings.

* Later, teach the use of *y* in words of Greek derivation, such as *cyclone*.

PREFIXES

During the intervening period, work on something else, perhaps Latin prefixes. These should be placed on three-by-five cards with the meanings on the reverse side. (See Figure 25.)

Figure 25.

front

back

Seven prefixes have changes that affect spelling. Teach these in pairs with their changes, as shown in Figure 26.

MISCELLANEOUS

Also continue work with spelling rules. Then add the rare long-vowel spellings so that the full list is as follows:

Figure 26.

con-* with/together—*congregate*
com before *m, p, b*—*commence, compel, combine*
col before *l*—*collide*
cor before *r*—*corrupt*
co before vowels—*coeducation*

in- in/not—*invade/inaccurate*
im before *m, p, b*—*immediate, impel, imbibe*
il before *l*—*illegal*
ir before *r*—*irregular*

dis- not/apart—*disobey/disintegrate*
di—*diverge*
dif before *f*—*differ*

ex- out—*exit*
e—*emerge*
ef before *f*—*effort*

sub- under—*submarine*
suc before *c*—*succeed*
suf before *f*—*suffer*
sup before *p*—*support*
also *suspect, suspend*

ob- against—*obstacle*
oc before *c*—*occur*
of before *f*—*offend*
op before *p*—*opponent*

ad- to/towards—*advance*
This prefix has ten changes, hence the many words with *a* followed by a double letter.
ac before *c, k, qu*—*accept, acknowledge, acquaint*
af before *f*—*affluent*
ag before *g*—*aggravate*
al before *l*—*allocate*
am before *m*—*ammunition*

an before *n*—*announce*
ap before *p*—*approach*
ar before *r*—*arrest*
as before *s*—*assist*
at before *t*—*attend*

---

* *Com-* is the correct form of the prefix, but for teaching purposes the form *con-* is convenient.

	Common				**Rare**		
a	a-e	ai	ay	ea	ei	eigh
e	e-e	ea	ee	ie	ei	
i	i-e	igh	y	y-e		
o	o-e	oa	ow	oe		
u	u-e	ue	ew	eu		

You can now tell the student he knows nearly all the sounds in the English language.

For the dyslexic, the diphthongs are confusing, and with good reason. Consider just these ten, which contain *o*:

oa—boat
oe—toe
oi—boil
oo—food
oo—book

ou—out
ou—soup
ow—cow
ow—snow
oy—boy

Difficult to sort out, too, are nine that contain *u* or *w*.

au—August
aw—saw
ou—out
ou—soup
ow—cow

ow—snow
ue—rescue
ew—few
eu—Europe

Learning long-vowel spellings thoroughly and reciting them frequently is an invaluable aid to establishing order in this confusion.

The tendency of the tongue to rise in the palate before a front vowel produces a set of particularly troublesome spellings.
• *ci* and *ti* are pronounced /sh/ as in *vicious* and *patient*.
• *du* is pronounced /jo͞o/ as in *individual*.

- *tu* is pronounced /chōo/ as in *virtuous*.

The Greek code is fun to teach, for reading as well as spelling.
- /f/ is spelled *ph* as in *phone*.
- /k/ is spelled *ch* as in *chrome*.
- /ĭ/ or /ī/ is spelled *y* as in *cyst, type,* and *phylum.* Any science textbook will provide plenty of examples.

Stable syllables with unchanging spelling include roots and suffixes (e.g., *ject, fect, ture, ent, ence, ity, ant, ance,* and *tain*) and need practice.

SPELLING RULES

Rules need to be kept to a minimum and taught in as simple a form as possible. Many can be introduced casually and drilled as needed.
- *Never* end a word in *v* (the Russians do it; we don't)—*have, love, give.*
- *Never* write *s* after *x* (the letter takes care of the *s*).
- *Always* put *u* after *q* (don't tell the student about *coq au vin* yet).
- If you hear *Q*, write *cu—peculiar.*
- If you hear *K*, write *ca—education.*
- If you heard *R*, write *ar—argument.*
- If you need an /er/ sound after *w*, use *or—work, worth, worship.*
- *w* and *qu* make *a* sound like *o—was, watch, quality, quantity.*
- Always use *m*, not *n*, before *p* and *b*.
- End nouns with *us*, adjectives with *ous—fungus, dangerous.*

Other rules require more formal teaching.

"Long spelling after short vowel." This is a useful rule with four applications. In the charts below, V stands for vowel and C stands for consonant. Note that if a consonant precedes the /ch/, /j/, or /k/ sound or a C*le* syllable, the short spelling is used regardless of the quality of the vowel, e.g., *bench, bilge, milk,* and *rumble.*

1.	V̆ + *tch*	V̄ or C + *ch*
	catch	coach
	hitch	teach
	notch	bench
	hutch	slouch
	fetch	starch
2.	V̆ + *dge*	V̄ or C + *ge*
	bridge	huge
	wedge	wage
	dodge	large
	fudge	bilge
	badge	stage

3.	V̆ + *ck*	V̄ or C + *k*
	tack	take
	snack	snake
	pick	pike
	deck	milk

The last one deals with the *consonant-le* syllable:

4.	V̆ + CC*le*	V̄ or C + C*le*
	saddle	bridle
	riddle	brindle
	ripple	rifle
	raffle	rumble

First have the student *tell* you in which column to place a word until you are sure he understands. Then, dictate words for him to place in the appropriate column. At first avoid exercises that require a student to insert *tch* or *ch* in a word that is partly written because such exercises are confusing. Use dictation or exercises that require the student to write the *entire* word.

Three rules have to do with the changes that occur when a suffix is added. Begin by teaching two kinds of suffixes.

Vowel Suffixes	Consonant Suffixes
-ed	-ly
-ing	-ful
-er	-ness
-est	-less
-ous	-ment
-y	etc.
etc.	

1. Silent-*e* Rule
   Words ending in silent *e*
   Drop the *e* before a vowel suffix
   Keep the *e* before a consonant suffix
   like + ing = liking
   like + ly = likely

2. Doubling Rule
   Words of *one* syllable
   ending in *one* consonant
   after *one* vowel (e.g., run, stop, slip)
   Double the final consonant before a vowel suffix
   run + ing = running
   stop + ed = stopped
   slip + er = slipper

3. Y Rule
   Never drop *y*
   Vowel + *y* (e.g., *ay, ey, oy, uy*)—keep the *y*
   employ + er = employer
   employ + ing = employing
   employ + ment = employment
   employ + able = employable

Consonant + *y* (e.g., *by, cy, dy, fy*)— change *y* to *i* unless the suffix begins with *i*

carry + ed = carried
carry + ing = carrying
happy + ness = happiness
happy + ly = happily
study + ed = studied
study + ing = studying

This rule differs from the preceding two in that the student must learn to look at the letter *before* the *y*.

There are other rules and generalizations that can be explored endlessly. Some are worth teaching, others are not. Always, the goal is to improve spelling: a few principles carefully taught and mastered are worth many more half-learned. As material on phonics or spelling rules is presented, it should be carefully organized in a notebook that the student keeps for reference.

PROOFREADING

Most of the mistakes the dyslexic makes are likely to be ones he could avoid by taking a second look. An instructive exercise is to tell a student to examine his writing and to compare the number of errors he can correct by himself with those he cannot. The discovery that only three of the fifteen errors on a page are "necessary" mistakes may inspire him to learn careful proofreading. Teachers are often surprised by the extent to which the dyslexic seems unable to see his mistakes—asked to read what he has written, he may repeatedly read what he *thinks* he has written, even omitting or inserting words and endings at will. The following activities have proved helpful:

1. Read it aloud.
2. Skip lines when writing so as to make the image clearer.
3. The teacher puts a mark indicating the presence of an error in the margin and the student finds the error.
4. The student underlines or, better, circles every word as he checks it.
5. The student goes over the paper in the same way, but backwards. This slows him down and makes him less likely to skip over a misspelling.

It must be remembered that there are stages in learning to spell a word. First, the student writes the word correctly when it is carefully pronounced for him by his teacher. Next, he spells it correctly in a single sentence. Providing practice for this stage is one of the many uses of sentence writing. Finally, the word becomes sufficiently established for him to spell it correctly in compositions when his mind is engaged in formulating his ideas.

THE DICTIONARY

One of the problems with using a dictionary is that if you cannot spell a word, you can't look it up. Various dictionaries for bad spellers have been devised, but their use is limited. For one thing, the authors cannot possibly conceive the many creative ways in which a dyslexic can misspell a word. Another problem is that the really poor speller seldom knows what to look up. He cannot tell which words are wrong and, short of looking up every single word, a hopelessly slow process, he has no recourse. Until spelling is at a fifth- or sixth-grade level, there is not much point in having a student struggle with a dictionary. It is better to simply supply words he needs or to have him form the habit of writing on and not worrying too much about the spelling of words he does not know. Last, for the dyslexic who has sequencing difficulties the system of alphabetical arrangement can be an insuperable obstacle, and this is the very student most in need of a dictionary. The most useful spelling dictionary for the dyslexic is the smallest—a vest pocket dictionary with a thumb-cut index.

7. Conclusion

The techniques described in this book have been developed in the course of thirty-five years of working with dyslexic adolescents. As the following writing samples demonstrate, these strategies have proved successful with students of diverse age, ability, and degree of difficulty. In all instances, the improvement has been dramatic. Students who could not compose a sentence write paragraphs; those struggling with single paragraphs write lengthy essays. They begin to write letters to friends and papers for their content courses and to enroll in college. Their handwriting may not be perfect, but it is serviceable—rapid and legible. Their spelling may not be accurate, but it no longer inhibits them.

What these writing samples cannot demonstrate is the concomitant gain in self-confidence that accompanies this freedom to write. For this reason, if for no other, the teaching process is always worth the effort. And effort it is, for both teacher and student. While the time elapsed between initial and final writing samples is brief, it is a period during which each student has written thousands of words and hundreds of sentences. Ease of writing comes through constant practice that forges new pathways through the brain in the fashion that is the essence of all learning.

Appendix

In all cases, students were seated in a classroom, supplied with pencils and paper and a list of topics or topic sentences from which to select, and given unlimited time, but no help whatsoever. Before-and-after samples are based on seven weeks of summer work or on a year or half a year of school work. In both cases, a daily tutoring session was scheduled, and ample study hall time was provided for practice.

Peter, a Westerner, aged thirty-three, had graduated from high school, started his own concrete business, and married. He left his business and family for the summer, and while even his final effort reflects profound dyslexia, at the end of seven weeks he was at least writing letters with confidence. On his return, he enrolled in a local community college and passed a course in psychology with a *B*.

Writing Sample 1.

6/83

I like to do conrten it is vary hard to do but I thik that it is good for me conrtiswhit

All writing samples have been reduced.

Writing Sample 2.

August 7, 1983

Jobs I Would Like To Have

I would like to be a coach of a baseball team. Because I like working with keds and boy making helppen them to grown and play as a team. Coaching is a inporten job you have to pick good plaer and to be a sumrt coah. You have to work the player very hard help them if they have iney prble. I like to see a chaponship team go all the way to state. Coaching would be a hard job to do but.

I also would like to be a big sickseceful business men in retale. And talk to all cines of pepol fome town to town. I would just like working with pepol in a business I could do a lot of fling. Because retale sounes fun is that going in a swoot would be neet to do. Most of all is that doing working to job I now have is a job. The concret business is a go time working around my help they work very hard for me and respet me. All and all working with pepol is what I like to do.

Ralph, aged twenty-two, had graduated from public school in special education classes. At the beginning of the summer, asked to write on *any* topic, he could not. The proctor's note read, "After *much* prodding I managed to get Ralph to write 4 objectives for summer camp (lots of frustration)." By the end of the summer his spelling and handwriting, though still poor, no longer prevented him from expressing his ideas.

Writing Sample 1.

6/26/83

rieding
writing
spilling
maths

Writing Sample 2.

August 7, 1983

Jous I Would Like to Have

In the fuecher I plan to open my own masonry bisness.
Jirstly il want to be my own boss. Because I don't like taking olders from people that yell all the time. My boss il work for now he work for two hour then he weast time talking to people. When he come back he yells that we didn't do any work all day long. Secintly the money is a lot bedder then six dollers and hour. We finish a foundation in three days, thats with pouring the floor to. He pays three of us $220 dollers for three days we make him $1600 dollers. We work hard all day long for cheep pay. Finuly il want to be my own boss becaue I would be making more money. I would pay my help what there worth.

Mark had graduated from high school, but his inability to write coherently made his prospects for a college worthy of his intelligence dim despite a score of 800 on the math section of his S.A.T. He had been diagnosed as dysgraphic, but the fact of the matter was that he had never learned correct letter formation of either lower- or uppercase letters. The second sample was written after five weeks of daily work.

Writing Sample 1.

9/14/81

It was the Science fair of 1977. I remember it well, It was with Jeneine that is. She was my girlfriend we had a project Based on the perfect conditions to have to Breed at fish in a Tank. you see the 'n. thonamous peter-yies' in her home oquarium at home had laid five eggs. god willingly just two weeks before the fair. but this is not important.

The most bewildering project, which I Thought the Best (if something can be the best and the most Stupid simotoneously) anyway. his name was Tim or Timothy Johnson to those who thought they new him; and couldn't realize that they didn't. he had set out to build a living person, but not only a living person, a beautiful Girl biology teacher to replace the nagging tyrant who enjoys the notation of our "O", the fifteeth letter in the Alphabet, with a flat left side on every report card. she had the privalage of giving me Several. besides an Eventual F and the usual There.

Writing Sample 2.

oct 23

Being an assistant counsellor at camp was the worst job I ever had. Since I was only an assistant counsellor, all the counsellors could give me orders. Once I had to sweep the entire gymnasium. I had been lying on the ground after two aggonizing, and exhausting baseball games. The basketball coach saw me and suspected me of wasting time. Before I knew it, he had me with a broom in my hand sweeping the floor. Another time, I was walking back to my bunk, and I happened to pass by the waterfront. The lifeguard called me down to the peir. I expected only to carry a few towels to the lost and found box. Instead, he had me get in the ice cold lake as a rescue victim for the campers trying for junior life saver. Also, the older campers often disobeyed my requests. On work day, I was asked to grab a few campers and move the ping pong tables into the messhall. I must have asked twenty campers, but all said they were busy. It took

Sally was eighteen and had graduated from high school, but her difficulty with written work prevented her from training to be a nurse. On both occasions she chose to write about relatives. The first composition is a sketchy paragraph; in the second one she makes her aunt come alive.

Writing Sample 1.

6/26/83

I had the opportunity to meet three of my grandparents. My grandparents on my father side and my ~~was~~ ~~gran~~ grandfather on my mothers side. My sister is named after my grandmother on my fathes side, her name is Donelda. I was named after my grandmother on my ~~for~~ mothers side, her ~~second~~ first name is Beatrice, my second. Two ~~of~~ of us were named after our grandparents.

Writing Sample 2.

Aug 10 / 83

The Most Unusuall Person

Who is the most unusual person you know? Mine would be my aunt, she is a very special person to me and my family. She is about eighty years old and lives by herself. she is very forgetfull, but, never fortgets a birth-day, or stories. Her home is cluttered with many trinkets and and old odds and sods she has picked up through her travels. One room is her chouse is full of pictures, all different kinds, most of them of people. One time I asked her about one of her pictures it was a man walking through the airport. She stopped and took the picture of him her reason she had funny looking shoes on. Another reason I picked to talk about my aunt is because of the stories she tells. Most of the time she picked out traits of our own doing and tells a story. At the end of the story we would all be in stitches because we could laugh about ourselfs Next and most import-and of all was when we were young she woued come over during a birthday party in a clown suit. The suit would have yellowish buttons down the

front and the biggest show floppiest shoes
ever seen. She was very rolly-polly
back then and when every we saw her
we would rush her to the ground. For many
years her name was Mrs. Clown because
nobody could pronnounce her real name.
Actually nobody knew her name til we
grew out of calling her Mrs. Clown. Her living
quarters, her stories will always be in
my mind but most of all the yellowish
buttons and the floppy feet will be imprint
ed and charished for ever.

Despite good intelligence, Todd had had a difficult time in school since first grade. When he was sixteen, he started in boarding school with daily tutoring. In the course of the year, he developed the ability to write a solid five-paragraph essay on almost any subject.

Writing Sample 1.

Sept. 18. 1984

I am very proad to be from the state of North Carolina. The state has many things to offer like It has a coast It also has mountains and a pedmont. Raleigh the capital is one of the fastest growing cities in the nation. The coast of N. C. is a great place to visite because of its sandbar party. and its grils. This concluds my report on my state

May 26, 1985

Value of Athletics

Athletics has a very important value in schools today. Beleive it or not alot can be acomplished through athletics. I feel there are three main reasons why athletics is and should be a part of every ~~shool~~ school. One is the fun in athletics, athletics gives a child a time to unwind from school. Two the fellowship in sports, the sports which are hard seem to make friend out of enemy. Third is the strees that comes with every day life; athletics help us forget our troubles.

The part of sports that people seem to like most is that its fun. Being fun has alot to to with why sports is good. If a sport is fun then the child plaing will have a much better time and all his aggestion will be taken care of. The child will go back to school all unwound and ready to study.

The fellowship in sports is very intense. Teammates would do almost anything for each other. If two teammates have a fight before a game and go into that game hating each other, by the end of the games they will be friends. Being on a team also lets you meet other people from other teams.

Life it self is full of stress + hatred and every day misfortunes. A man with all that on his shoulders is on the verge of a breakdown. Sports would be a great way to forget and have a great time. Sports will keep you from here a bad day.

These are three main reasons why I feel that sports are a big deal. Sports has alot to offer and a wide range of different things to do. The old saying saying says it the best "All work and no play makes Jack a dull boy."

At fifteen, Marty used the phrase, "That's all I remember," twice in his initial paragraph. In his final effort, at the end of the summer, he chose to tackle a comparison/contrast topic. While his success was limited, the improvement is marked.

Writing Sample 1.

June 24, 1984

My grandparents is giving me a Celica Supra. The car has an atomic shift, a F.M., AM and casset radio, a sun roof, a great air conditioner, cruse control, and speedometer + odometer. That all I remember about the inside. The car is a blue with a red line, and its a door veacale. That all I remember.

Writing Sample 2.

July 27, 1984

Houston vs. Amenia

I have been to both Houston and Amenia and there are some big differents between them. First of all, Houston has a enormous population. It has a population of almost 2 million. Amenia is a small town with probable a couple of thousand people. In the noisy area, Houston is loud and very active while Amenia is a quiet place. Also, Houston is the number 1 area for car accidents. Amenia doesn't have many accidents which will happen. But Houston has great amusements than Amenia. Houston has parks, Go carts, water bumper cars, putt putt golf areas, Astroworld, Waterworld, golf, a zoo and others while Amenia just has parks and theater.

Houston has thing to do at like discos, theaters, concerts, sports, and amusement parks. Amenia has only a theater to watch movies at night. Finally, Houston has a pollution problem that pretty bad. Amenia has a little pollution but it do much harm to the people. If I had to choose one of those places to live in, I would pick Houston.

Dustin, a Canadian fifteen year old with a full-scale intelligence quotient of 144, was failing nearly everything in school. His "dysgraphia" had been diagnosed early and he had had some help with his handwriting. However, he retained an aversion to writing and an unwillingness to put anything down on paper. By the end of a summer's tutoring, he was beginning to enjoy expressing his ideas.

Writing Sample 1.

> June 24 84
>
> Sorry this will be short. I dont write. my sole form of writin comunication is doodle and poetry. If you like Ill just hand in some pictures.

August 5 1984

Rock Bands

The Quiet Side to Being Loud

Eight years ago Malcom Mclaren exposed to the world the future. He had gotten together his greatest effort in music within the span of his career. Malcom called them "The Sex Pistols", and they were the forerunners of punk rock. They were the idols of British press and they sold in excess of one million pounds in their short career. Although each had a violent exterior, due to the touchy subjects the sung of, the Sex Pistols were plainly the exsamples of a overlooked society in the U.K. Jhonny Rotten was a Talentless drop-out who was known for his radical political views, (Wich were soon to be the views of British youth) and his chalky speaking voice. Sid Vicious, on the other hand, was quieter, but was an acomplied barroom brawler, and had a drug habit that caused his, and, conciquently, the bands early demise. They sung of abortions, anarchy, endangered animals, and, in thier review, the facisim of monarchy's. They were mistaken for violent idiots who didnt have any idea of what they spoke of, but they truly the begginning of the age of awareness in music. For without the Sex Pistols and punk rock, we would still be waiting for instant Uttopia. We would not know of the "Young Orwelians" or the poverty that kills in all places. Thanks to punk rock, we, the youth of the world, have a message of peace and realization in our most popular media.

When Alan was twelve he started boarding school late, in the middle of the year. Even so, the contrast between his January and May paragraphs is striking.

Writing Sample 1.

Jan.¼ - 83

This paragraph is about video games. Video games are very exciting if your playing it. If your not they are kind of exciting. To play a game you would have to put a token in the game.

Writing Sample 2.

May 30, 1983

This spring the Juniors took several insteresting field trips. One is we went to a farm and saw different kinds of animals like cows, horses, chickens, roosters and bulls. We saw the men milking cows and feeding horses. We also went on cookouts and we had hot dog and hamburger and all different kinds of food. We went to the pond and to the forest also. Once we went to a farm and they should us draf horses that pull weights. Sometimes we went to get modils at a store in pokipsi or at Ames plaza. Once we went to a river and fished there for a while or we went to a lake in lakerville or we went to another place and fished there or we swimmed and played around Another place we went to was a ski jump where they pratice Jumping. We climb up to the top and you could see for miles around and we saw America.

We went camping on one of are field trips and it was fun.
We told ghost stories and we whent swimming and fishing. we
went to the Alpin slide but it was closed so we walk up it.

Although he was eleven and full of ideas, Joseph had never learned cursive writing. Six weeks of tutoring enabled him to produce a reasonably fluent and age-appropriate paragraph.

Writing Sample 1.

June 24
1984

what you Need to play Dungons and Dragons

Dungons and Dragons is a fantasy adventure game. to play Dungons and Dragons (D&D) you need Dice (4 sided, 6 sided, 8 sided, 10 sided, 12 sided, and 20 sided) and an expereanced Dungon master (DM) and some payers

Writing Sample 2.

July 13, 1984

Christmas is my favorite holiday for several reasons. First, I like Christmas because I am Christian. I like the church service on Chistmas Eve. It is a wonderful ecation because we are sellabrating the birth of Christ. Next, my birth day is right after it. I get tons of Christmas presants and then right after I get tons more for my birthday. That mean I get twice as much before I grow out of the fist batch. Finally, I like to give gifts. I like to give gifts because the other person will give me a gift back. I also like to make people happy. This is why I love Chistmas.

At ten, Doug was more comfortable drawing than writing, but by the end of a year, what later developed into a knack for original expression was beginning to show.

Writing Sample 1.

Sept. 13 1982

♡VIDEO GAMES

the New video game out now that is sweeping the country is donkey Kong. The Object is to save the girl from the monkey. You climb up matle like poles and and latters latters until you save the girl. Once you save the girl You go on to different boords and try to save the girl.

Atari came out with the game donkey kong and also did intelevision. The reason why it is so good is the graphics.

monkeygirl ↓ ONE of the boords

Writing Sample 2.

December 8, 1982

I can't wait for the first snowfall.
The first snow falls usually bettween
Thanksgiving and Christmas. The first snow
fall sometimes closes schools, because the high-
way maintance doen't clear the roads as fast
as they would, and people are very causious.
In addition, the first snow fall causes more car
acidents, and more people die because of careless
driving. Also, the hardware business starts to pick
up, people buying snow shovels, and snow blowers,
and equipment needed for snow When it snows
more toward Christmas people turn on there
lights on their trees. That makes a great effect
at night a white blanket of snow and all the
colorful lights. The first snow fall brings
children out to make snowmen, and have snow
ball fights, and great fun all over.

When he was nine years old, John was having so much difficulty in school that his parents decided to enroll him in the boarding school program. He stayed for a second year, but even by the end of the first year, his progress was evident.

Writing Sample 1.

I have a box and in it is a hat.   12-2-81

Writing Sample 2.

jun 2, 1982

fishing is my favorite summer sport.
I like too go on boad and too cach the fish.
I put on miy hucs and I use sultimes..
I use a fly. and the time to go fish is.
4.0 0 okloc and I usule go too the ponds.
and I got bror bass and suft wother and
I have got sunes and too bee prord too
coch the fish the end o

Susan was only eight, but a summer of tutoring enabled her to begin learning to organize and expand her ideas.

Writing Sample 1.

> June 25, 1984
>
> One day there was a littil girl
> she was so hoppy.
> Becus she was Byeing a Ritin.
> wen she got it she spened moste
> uf her time with it.
> It was rel fun the
>
> the End

Writing Sample 2.

Aug. 10, 1984

There are several reasons why I like the dogs at camp. First of all, I like them because they are fun to play with. I like to chase Sky. Second of all, I like the dogs at camp because they always follow around. Last of all, I like the dogs at camp because they are cute and friendly. I am going to miss all of them when I leave camp..

Selected Bibliography

The following is my list of most valuable books for teachers working to improve the writing skills of the adolescent.

Decker, Randall E. *Decker's Patterns of Exposition,* Vol. 9. Boston: Little, Brown and Company, 1984.

This is a wonderful selection of essays illustrating different kinds of expository writing. The selections are varied and interesting, but the material is geared to the advanced student.

Gillingham, Anna, and Stillman, Bessie W. *Remedial Training for Children with Specific Disability in Reading, Spelling, and Penmanship.* Cambridge, MA: Educators Publishing Service, Inc., 1960.

This classic is a wonderful resource. The Red edition is probably more useful than the later Green one. Especially valuable is the section on long-vowel spellings.

Langan, John. *English Skills.* Second Edition. New York: McGraw-Hill Book Company, 1981.

The best single book for teaching adolescents to write that I have come across. The exercises are full of humor and every point is aptly illustrated. For the dyslexic, the material profits from some rearranging. Included are good sections on sentence structure and on punctuation.

Langan, John. *Sentence Skills.* New York: McGraw-Hill Book Company, 1979.

A useful approach to writing better sentences, this book does not rely on the student's knowledge of formal grammar.

Rak, Elsie T. *Spellbound, The Spell of Words,* and *Spellbinding.* Cambridge, MA: Educators Publishing Service, Inc., 1981, 1980, and 1978.

A useful series of workbooks on phonics and spelling.

Riddlesbarger, Ada, and Stillwagon, Nell. *Easy English Exercises.* San Diego: Harcourt Brace Jovanovich, 1956.

An excellent grammar book, this hardback text contains plenty of exercises and examples.

Strunk, William, Jr., and White, E.B. *The Elements of Style.* New York: Macmillan Publishing Co., Inc., 1979.

Probably of more value to the teacher interested in improving his or her own knowledge of syntax and word usage than to the student.

Steere, Amey; Peck, Caroline Z.; and Kahn, Linda. *Solving Language Difficulties.* Cambridge, MA: Educators Publishing Service, Inc., 1971.

For the adolescent, this is the single most helpful workbook on spelling.

Treanor, John H. *Exercises in English Grammar,* Books I and II. Cambridge, MA: Educators Publishing Service, Inc., 1963 and 1972.

This is an elementary introduction to grammar with plenty of exercises.

Wood, Earl F. *Junior English Review Exercises,* Books I and II, and *Senior English Review Exercises.* Cambridge, MA: Educators Publishing Service, Inc., 1980, 1979, and 1980.

This series includes some challenging exercises on clauses, verbals, and syntax. Unless you are very sure of yourself, obtain an answer key and practice the exercises yourself first; they are relatively difficult.